ASIA BOND MONITOR
SEPTEMBER 2024

ASIAN DEVELOPMENT BANK

ADB

© 2024 Asian Development Bank
6 ADB Avenue, Mandaluyong City, 1550 Metro Manila, Philippines
Tel +63 2 8632 4444; Fax +63 2 8636 2444
www.adb.org

Some rights reserved. Published in 2024.

ISBN 978-92-9270-871-9 (print); 978-92-9270-872-6 (PDF); 978-92-9270-873-3 (ebook)
ISSN 2219-1518 (print), 2219-1526 (PDF)
Publication Stock No. SGP240417-2
DOI: http://dx.doi.org/10.22617/SGP240417-2

The views expressed in this publication are those of the authors and do not necessarily reflect the views and policies of the Asian Development Bank (ADB) or its Board of Governors or the governments they represent.

ADB does not guarantee the accuracy of the data included in this publication and accepts no responsibility for any consequence of their use. The mention of specific companies or products of manufacturers does not imply that they are endorsed or recommended by ADB in preference to others of a similar nature that are not mentioned.

By making any designation of or reference to a particular territory or geographic area in this document, ADB does not intend to make any judgments as to the legal or other status of any territory or area.

Please contact pubsmarketing@adb.org if you have questions or comments with respect to content, or if you wish to obtain copyright permission for your intended use that does not fall within these terms, or for permission to use the ADB logo.

Corrigenda to ADB publications may be found at http://www.adb.org/publications/corrigenda.

Note:
ADB recognizes "China" as the People's Republic of China; "Hong Kong" as Hong Kong, China; "Korea" as the Republic of Korea; "Siam" as Thailand; and "Vietnam" as Viet Nam.

Cover design by Erickson Mercado.

Contents

Emerging East Asian Local Currency Bond Markets: A Regional Update

Executive Summary

Recent Developments in Financial Conditions in Emerging East Asia

During the review period of 1 June–30 August, financial conditions in emerging East Asia improved over expectations of policy rate cuts in both advanced economies and regional markets amid the continued moderation of inflation.[1] The improvement largely started in July when the United States (US) Federal Reserve hinted at a likely policy rate cut in September. This led to the overall decline of bond yields in both advanced and regional markets during the review period. There was a brief overreaction in financial markets in early August following the release of weak US labor market data and related concerns over a possible recession, which heightened investor risk aversion. Financial markets subsequently corrected, with financial conditions continuing to improve through the rest of the review period.

During the review period, regional financial indicators showed improved performance. Regional currencies collectively appreciated against the US dollar by 3.3% (simple average) and 2.7% (gross-domestic-product-weighted). Risk premiums, as measured by credit default swap spreads, narrowed by 7.4 basis points (simple average) and 5.2 basis points (gross-domestic-product-weighted). However, while regional equity markets gained by 2.4% (simple average), they recorded marginal losses of 3.7% (market-weighted) over weakness in the People's Republic of China's (PRC) economic performance. Excluding the PRC and Hong Kong, China, the region's equity markets gained 4.3% (simple average) and 3.6% (market-weighted). Regional equity markets recorded net portfolio inflows of USD7.6 billion during the review period.

Risks to the outlook for regional financial conditions were broadly balanced. On the upside, a global moderation in inflation and forthcoming rate cuts by central banks could further strengthen financial conditions. Downside risks include geopolitical concerns, a weaker-than-expected economic performance in the PRC, trade tensions between the US and the PRC, as well as recent domestic uncertainty in some Association of Southeast Asian Nations (ASEAN) markets. Regional financial conditions may also be subject to market volatility in response to negative news, similar to what was observed in early August.

Recent Developments in Local Currency Bond Markets in Emerging East Asia

The emerging East Asian local currency (LCY) bond market expanded 2.3% quarter-on-quarter (q-o-q) and 9.2% year-on-year (y-o-y) in the second quarter (Q2) of 2024, totaling USD25.1 trillion at the end of June. Quarterly growth in the region's LCY bonds outstanding in Q2 2024 accelerated from 1.4% q-o-q in the first quarter (Q1) of 2024, supported by faster expansions of Treasury and corporate bonds. Treasury bonds outstanding expanded 2.8% q-o-q in Q2 2024, up from 1.3% q-o-q in the prior quarter, as the PRC increased issuance of sovereign bonds to finance stimulus measures. Meanwhile, growth in the region's corporate bond market rose to 1.5% q-o-q in Q2 2024 from 1.2% q-o-q in Q1 2024 on increased issuance in six of the region's nine markets, led by the PRC where banks ramped up debt sales to meet regulatory capital requirements. Aggregate LCY bonds outstanding in ASEAN markets reached USD2.2 trillion at the end of June and accounted for an 8.9% share of the region's total.

LCY bond issuance in emerging East Asia rebounded in Q2 2024, supported by expansions in both the government and corporate bond segments. Quarterly LCY bond issuance reached USD2.6 trillion at the end of June, posting 15.4% q-o-q growth in Q2 2024 following a 9.1% q-o-q contraction in the prior quarter. Treasury bond issuance expanded 27.0% q-o-q in Q2 2024 to

[1] Emerging East Asia is defined to include member states of the Association of Southeast Asian Nations plus the People's Republic of China; Hong Kong, China; and the Republic of Korea.

USD1.1 trillion, fueled by the PRC's accelerated issuance of local and long-term Treasury bonds intended to support the economy. Issuance of LCY corporate bonds (USD860.9 billion) rebounded in Q2 2024, rising 5.6% q-o-q after a 1.9% q-o-q dip in Q1 2024, as the PRC and most ASEAN markets posted higher corporate debt sales. Strong corporate bond issuance in the PRC was driven by banks raising funds to meet regulatory requirements, while most ASEAN markets recorded increased issuance on improved financial conditions. ASEAN markets' combined issuance of LCY bonds tallied USD602.4 billion in Q2 2024, comprising 23.6% of the region's total.

Emerging East Asian Treasury bonds outstanding and issuance in Q2 2024 were largely concentrated in medium- to long-term maturities. At the end of June, over half of outstanding Treasury bonds (52.6%) and newly issued Treasury bonds (55.9%) had remaining maturities of over 5 years. The size-weighted average tenor of the region's outstanding Treasury bonds was 8.6 years at the end of June, while the size-weighted average tenor of Treasury bonds issued in Q2 2024 was 9.5 years.

Banks and insurance companies continued to hold the largest shares of emerging East Asian LCY bonds. At the end of June, banks held an average share of 36.2% of outstanding LCY bonds in the region, followed by insurance companies with 28.9%.

Recent Developments in ASEAN+3 Sustainable Bond Markets

The sustainable bond market in ASEAN+3 posted a robust annual expansion of 17.4% to reach a size of USD868.1 billion at the end of June.[2] The y-o-y growth of ASEAN+3's outstanding sustainable bonds outpaced corresponding growth in both the European Union 20 (EU-20) (16.5%) and the global (17.0%) sustainable bond markets. A high volume of maturities during the quarter, however, led to q-o-q growth moderating to 1.9% in Q2 2024 from 2.9% in Q1 2024. Within ASEAN+3, ASEAN economies posted the region's fastest growth at 6.4% q-o-q on higher issuance volumes. ASEAN+3 remained the world's second-largest regional sustainable bond market, accounting for 19.0% of the global

sustainable bond market at the end of June, following the EU-20's 36.9%. Despite its continued expansion, however, the ASEAN+3 sustainable bond market comprised only 2.3% of the region's total bond market at the end of Q2 2024, which was less than the EU-20 sustainable bond market's 7.8%.

Sustainable bond issuance rebounded in Q2 2024 to USD51.0 billion on a 1.6% q-o-q expansion after contracting 10.7% q-o-q in the prior quarter. ASEAN+3 accounted for 23.1% of the global issuance in Q2 2024. LCY-denominated sustainable bonds accounted for 79.3% of ASEAN+3's total issuance for the quarter, compared with an LCY issuance share of 94.7% in the region's general bond market. About 69.6% of ASEAN+3's sustainable bond issuance in Q2 2024 was financed by short-term maturities (tenors of less than 5 years). Shorter-tenor financing was more prevalent in sustainable bond issuance among non-ASEAN economies (74.4%), while longer-tenor issuances (over 5 years) were more dominant among ASEAN markets (70.6%). In Q2 2024, the size-weighted average tenor of ASEAN+3 sustainable bond issuance was 6.9 years, lagging the corresponding averages in the EU-20 sustainable bond market (9.6 years) and the ASEAN+3 general bond market (8.7 years). ASEAN economies had a longer size-weighted average tenor of 18.0 years, owing to the active participation of the public sector in ASEAN markets.

---

[2] ASEAN+3 is defined to include member states of ASEAN plus the People's Republic of China; Hong Kong, China; Japan; and the Republic of Korea.

Developments in Regional Financial Conditions

Financial conditions in emerging East Asia improved from 1 June to 30 August over expectations of policy rate cuts in both advanced economies and regional markets amid the continued moderation of inflation.[1] Most of the improvements started in July when the United States (US) Federal Reserve hinted that a policy rate cut was likely in September. Expected policy rate cuts in the US and the euro area drove down bond yields in both advanced and regional markets during the review period (**Table A**). The expectation of rate cuts also contributed to the collective appreciation of regional currencies against the US dollar and a decline in risk premiums. Most regional equity markets posted gains leading to capital inflows during the review period, as investor confidence was restored following the short-lived market turmoil in early August. The market turmoil was largely driven by dampened investor sentiment over the weakening US labor market and related concerns about a possible recession. Risks to the financial conditions outlook are balanced over the next quarter. On the upside, moderating inflation and an end to monetary tightening in the region could contribute to the

further improvement of financial conditions. Downside risks include rising geopolitical risks, recent domestic uncertainty in some Association of Southeast Asian Nations (ASEAN) markets, trade tensions between the US and the People's Republic of China (PRC), a weaker-than-expected economic performance in the PRC, and uncertainty regarding the US election. Regional financial conditions are also exposed to market volatility from negative news, such as the financial turmoil experienced in early August.

Bond yields fell in the US during the review period over a widely expected Federal Reserve rate cut in September amid moderating inflation and some signs of economic weakness. During the 11–12 June Federal Open Market Committee (FOMC) meeting, the Federal Reserve left the federal funds target rate unchanged and acknowledged progress toward its 2.0% inflation goal. During the 30–31 July FOMC meeting, the Federal Reserve left its policy rate unchanged, while confirming further progress toward achieving its inflation goal. The Federal Reserve

Table A: Changes in Financial Conditions in Major Advanced Economies and Select Emerging East Asian Markets from 1 June to 30 August 2024

	2-Year Government Bond Yield (bps)	10-Year Government Bond Yield (bps)	5-Year Credit Default Swap Spread (bps)	Equity Index (%)	FX Rate (%)
Major Advanced Economies					
Euro Area	(71)	(37)	–	(0.5)	1.8
Japan	(3)	(17)	(2)	(1.7)	7.6
United States	(96)	(60)	–	7.0	–
Select Emerging East Asian Markets					
People's Republic of China	(24)	(15)	(5)	(7.9)	2.1
Hong Kong, China	(109)	(94)	–	(0.5)	0.3
Indonesia	(26)	(26)	(5)	10.0	5.1
Republic of Korea	(40)	(49)	(4)	1.4	3.5
Malaysia	(23)	(13)	(9)	5.1	8.9
Philippines	(30)	(68)	(9)	7.2	4.3
Singapore	(87)	(65)	–	3.2	3.4
Thailand	(19)	(27)	(7)	1.0	8.6
Viet Nam	(0.4)	(13)	(14)	1.8	2.3

( ) = negative, – = not available, bps = basis points, FX = foreign exchange.

Note: FX rates are presented against the United States dollar. A positive (negative) value for the FX rate indicates the appreciation (depreciation) of the local currency against the United States dollar.

Source: *AsianBondsOnline* calculations based on Bloomberg LP data.

---

[1] Emerging East Asia is defined to include member states of the Association of Southeast Asian Nations plus the People's Republic of China; Hong Kong, China; and the Republic of Korea.

also noted at the July meeting that unemployment had risen slightly and job gains had moderated. With both inflation and the job market's performance supporting a rate cut, Federal Reserve Chair Jerome Powell hinted that the Federal Reserve would cut interest rates at its next FOMC meeting in September unless inflation progress stalled. While the weaker labor market performance data released on 2 August triggered a market overreaction on fears that this was a looming sign of recession, this concern has since abated. Based on the CME FedWatch tool, on 31 July, markets were pricing an 11.8% probability of a 50 basis points (bps) rate cut at the September meeting; this probability surged to 85.0% on 5 August following the release of weak labor market data on 2 August. Meanwhile, the probability of a 25 bps rate cut in September fell from 88.1% on 31 July to 15.0% on 5 August.

In August, Federal Reserve officials helped set market expectations. San Francisco Federal Reserve President Mary Daly said on 5 August that the job market was softening but remained sound and that companies were merely slowing their hiring and not cutting jobs. On the same day, Chicago Federal Reserve President Austan Goolsbee said that the recent jobs report was not necessarily a recession indicator and that the Federal Reserve was looking at the totality of the data. During the 22–24 August Jackson Hole symposium, Federal Reserve Chair Jerome Powell indicated that "the time has come for policy to adjust." In his speech, Jerome Powell noted that the labor market had weakened while inflation was on a sustainable downward trend. By 30 August, the probability of a 50 bps rate cut at the September meeting had plunged to 30.0%, while the probability of a 25 bps rate cut had risen to 70.0%. The probabilities of 25 bps rate cuts at the November and December FOMC meetings also rose to 49.3% and 30.0%, respectively, on 30 August, from 21.1% and 14.0% on 3 June (**Figure A**).

The US economy remained sound but witnessed some signs of weakness during the review period. At the June FOMC meeting, the Federal Reserve kept its 2024 forecasts for annualized gross domestic product (GDP) growth and the unemployment rate unchanged at 2.1% and 4.0%, respectively, the same as its March forecasts. But projected annual Personal Consumption Expenditures (PCE) inflation for 2024 was revised slightly higher to 2.6% from 2.4% in March. Second estimates for second quarter (Q2) US GDP showed annualized growth

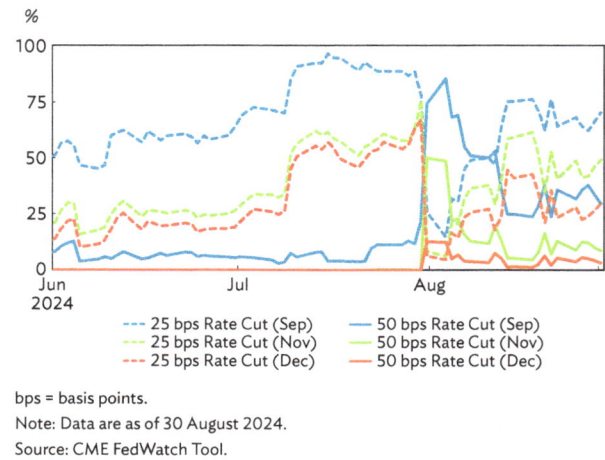

Figure A: Probability of a 25 Basis Points versus a 50 Basis Points Rate Cut at the September, November, and December Federal Open Market Committee Meetings

bps = basis points.
Note: Data are as of 30 August 2024.
Source: CME FedWatch Tool.

of 3.0%, up from 1.4% in the previous quarter, driven by improved consumer spending and business sentiment. Headline inflation continued to trend downward, clocking in at 2.9% year-on-year (y-o-y) in July from 3.0% y-o-y in June and 3.3% y-o-y in May. July's print was the first time since March 2021 that consumer price inflation had fallen below 3.0% y-o-y. PCE inflation also ticked down to 2.5% y-o-y in June and July from 2.6% y-o-y in May, while core PCE inflation (excluding energy and food) was steady at 2.6% y-o-y in May, June, and July. Overall business activity remained in an expansionary regime, as evidenced by composite Purchasing Managers Index (PMI) readings of 54.8, 54.3, and 54.6 in June, July, and August, respectively, as well as services PMI readings of 55.3, 55.0, and 55.7, respectively. However, the manufacturing PMI fell further to 47.9 in August from 49.6 in July and 51.6 in June. The July reading was below the expansionary threshold of 50.0 for the first time this year, indicating softening in the manufacturing sector. Labor market indicators continued showing some weakness. Nonfarm payroll additions read 142,000 in August, higher than 89,000 in July and 118,000 in June, but lower than the expected 160,000. The unemployment rate in the US dropped slightly to 4.2% in August from 4.3% in July, the highest since October 2021, but was still up from 4.1% in June.

In the euro area, government bond yields fell during the review period following the European Central Bank's (ECB) policy rate cut in June. The ECB reduced its key policy rates by 25 bps during its 5–6 June meeting but stressed that it was not pre-committing to a particular rate path. At its 17–18 July meeting, the ECB kept its key policy rates steady, noting that the June policy rate cut had been transmitted smoothly. After the July meeting, some ECB officials hinted at a possible rate cut in the September meeting. On 22 July, ECB Governing Council member Peter Kazimir said that market expectations of two rate cuts this year were not "misplaced," but the ECB would continue to assess incoming data. On 25 July, Deutsche Bundesbank President Joachim Nagel indicated that the ECB would cut rates if economic data lined up with previous forecasts. Bank of Portugal Vice Governor Clara Raposo mentioned that the ECB could cut rates twice this year provided that inflation fell within expectations. On 23 August, Bank of Portugal Governor Mario Centeno said that a September cut was an "easy decision." However, some members remained cautious. De Nederlandsche Bank President Klaas Knot indicated on 27 August that he wanted more data before deciding on a September cut. On 29 August, Joachim Nagel mentioned that while the euro area was close to its inflation target, it was important not to cut rates too quickly.

Meanwhile, the euro area's economic recovery remained fragile. Economic conditions saw improvements during the review period as the euro area's GDP growth rose to 0.6% y-o-y in Q2 2024 from 0.5% y-o-y in the previous quarter. The ECB's June 2024 GDP forecast was raised to 0.9% y-o-y from 0.6% y-o-y in March. The euro area's composite PMI improved slightly to 51.0 in August from 50.2 in July, and the services PMI rose to 52.9 from 51.9 over the same period. However, some underlying weakness remained. The manufacturing PMI remained below the 50-point expansion threshold in August at 45.8, the same as in both June and July. Meanwhile, euro area inflation eased to 2.2% y-o-y in August from 2.6% y-o-y and 2.5% y-o-y in July and June, respectively. The ECB's inflation forecast for 2024 was raised to 2.5% y-o-y in June from 2.3% y-o-y in March.

In Japan, 2-year and 10-year bond yields fell during the review period despite the Bank of Japan's (BOJ) 15 bps rate hike at its 31 July meeting. The decline in bond yields happened mostly during early August's market turmoil, when losses in Japanese equity markets spurred risk aversion and increased demand for safer Japanese government bonds. Losses in equity markets were driven by asset sales, when investors unwound their Japanese yen carry trade positions on the increased

likelihood of faster-than-expected US rate cuts. At its 31 July meeting, the BOJ hiked the policy rate for a second time in 2024, citing that growth and inflation were generally in line with the central bank's outlook. The BOJ also signaled the possibility of further monetary policy normalization. The central bank announced plans to reduce its Japanese government bond purchases, beginning in August, by about JPY400 billion each quarter until its monthly purchases decline to about JPY2.9 trillion by the first quarter of 2026. On 1 August, BOJ Governor Kazuo Ueda said that he still deemed real interest rates to be low. Market participants are expecting another rate hike this year as the BOJ reported in its 31 July statement that "if the outlook for economic activity and prices presented in the July Outlook Report will be realized, the BOJ will accordingly continue to raise the policy interest rate and adjust the degree of monetary accommodation." Also, on 22 August, Kazuo Ueda reiterated that the BOJ would raise rates if its economic forecasts are met.

During the review period, the Japanese economy improved on a strong performance in Q2 2024. GDP growth (seasonally adjusted annualized rate) rebounded to 2.9% in Q2 2024, buoyed by rising consumption. Inflation remained above the 2.5% y-o-y target in both July and June at 2.8% y-o-y, up from 2.5% y-o-y in April. Consumer sentiment in Japan showed signs of improvement. The composite PMI rose to 52.9 in August (an 8-month high) from 52.5 in July and 49.7 in June, while the services PMI improved to 53.7 in July from 49.4 in June and remained at this level in August. However, the manufacturing PMI remained in a contractionary regime (albeit with some improvement), with an August reading of 49.8, up from 49.1 in July. The Japanese job market remained sound, as the unemployment rate stood at 2.5% and 2.7% in June and July, respectively, a similar level to 2.6% in May. At its July meeting, however, the BOJ revised downward its 2024 inflation forecast to 2.5% y-o-y from the April forecast of 2.8% y-o-y. The BOJ's fiscal year 2024 growth forecast was revised downward to 0.6% y-o-y in July from 0.8% y-o-y in April.

Local currency bond yields fell for both 2-year and 10-year tenors in all emerging East Asian markets, following continued moderation in domestic inflation and lower bond yields in advanced markets. Inflation continued its moderating trend in most regional markets during the review period (**Figure B**). The Philippines and Viet Nam, which posted relatively higher inflation in the region in July, saw their respective inflation

Figure B: Inflation in Major Advanced Economies and Select Emerging East Asian Markets

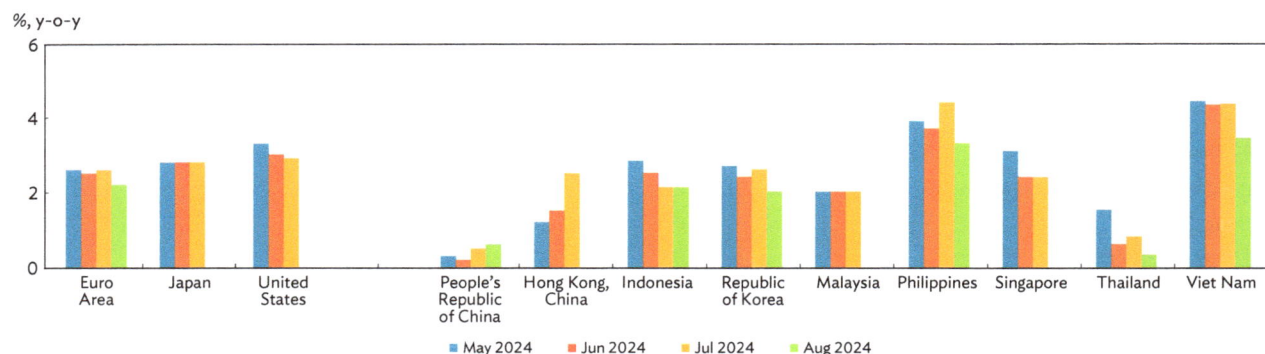

%, y-o-y

■ May 2024   ■ Jun 2024   ■ Jul 2024   ■ Aug 2024

y-o-y = year-on-year.
Note: Data coverage is from May to August 2024 except for Hong Kong, China; Japan; Malaysia; Singapore; and the United States (July 2024).
Sources: Various local sources.

Table B: Changes in Monetary Stances in Major Advanced Economies and Select Emerging East Asian Markets

Economy	Policy Rate 1-Aug-2023 (%)	Rate Change (%)													Policy Rate 30-Aug-2024 (%)	Change in Policy Rates (basis points)
		Aug-2023	Sep-2023	Oct-2023	Nov-2023	Dec-2023	Jan-2024	Feb-2024	Mar-2024	Apr-2024	May-2024	Jun-2024	Jul-2024	Aug-2024		
Euro Area	3.50	↑0.25	↑0.25									↓0.25			3.75	↑ 25
Japan	(0.10)								↑0.20				↑0.15		0.25	↑ 35
United Kingdom	5.00	↑0.25												↓0.25	5.00	◆ 0
United States	5.50														5.50	◆ 0
People's Republic of China	2.65	↓0.15											↓0.20		2.30	↓ 35
Indonesia	5.75			↑0.25						↑0.25					6.25	↑ 50
Republic of Korea	3.50														3.50	◆ 0
Malaysia	3.00														3.00	◆ 0
Philippines	6.25			↑0.25										↓0.25	6.25	◆ 0
Singapore	–														–	–
Thailand	2.00	↑0.25	↑0.25												2.50	↑ 50
Viet Nam	4.50														4.50	◆ 0

( ) = negative, ◆ = no change, – = no data.
Notes:
1. Data coverage is from 1 August 2023 to 30 August 2024.
2. For the People's Republic of China, the data used in the chart are for the 1-year medium-term lending facility rate. While the 1-year benchmark lending rate is the official policy rate of the People's Bank of China, market players use the 1-year medium-term lending facility rate as a guide for the bank's monetary policy direction.
3. For the United States, the upper bound of the policy rate target range is reported on the table.
4. The up (down) arrow for Singapore signifies monetary policy tightening (loosening) by its central bank. The Monetary Authority of Singapore utilizes the Singapore dollar nominal effective exchange rate to guide its monetary policy.
Sources: Various central bank websites.

rates moderating to 3.3% y-o-y (from 4.4% y-o-y) and 3.5% y-o-y (from 4.4% y-o-y) in August due to slower increases in food prices. The decline in yields in the region was also influenced by market expectations of more rate cuts in both advanced economies and the region. During the review period, most central banks in emerging East Asia held their policy rates unchanged (**Table B**). The exceptions were the PRC and the Philippines; both conducted rate cuts. On 22 July, the People's Bank of China (PBOC) surprisingly reduced by

10 bps each the 7-day repurchase rate, the 1-year loan prime rate, and the 5-year loan prime rate. The PBOC's rate cut was to support economic activities as Q2 2024 GDP fell to 4.7% y-o-y from 5.3% y-o-y in the first quarter. On 25 July, the PBOC lowered the 1-year medium-term lending facility rate by 20 bps to 2.3%. On 15 August, the Bangko Sentral ng Pilipinas lowered its policy rate by 25 bps. The central bank indicated that inflation is expected to fall within its 2024 target range of 2.0%–4.0%. Some central banks have signaled their planned rate

Table C: Gross Domestic Product Growth in Select Emerging East Asian Economies (%, y-o-y)

Economy	2024		
	Q1	Q2	Forecast
People's Republic of China	5.30	4.70	4.80
Hong Kong, China	2.80	3.30	2.80
Indonesia	5.11	5.05	5.00
Republic of Korea	3.30	2.30	2.50
Malaysia	4.20	5.90	4.50
Philippines	5.80	6.30	6.00
Singapore	3.00	2.90	2.40
Thailand	1.60	2.30	2.60
Viet Nam	5.66	6.93	6.00

Q1 = first quarter, Q2 = second quarter, y-o-y = year-on-year.
Note: Forecasts for 2024 are based on the *Asian Development Outlook July 2024*.
Sources: Various local sources.

Figure C: Currency Exchange Rate Against the United States Dollar in Select Emerging East Asian Markets

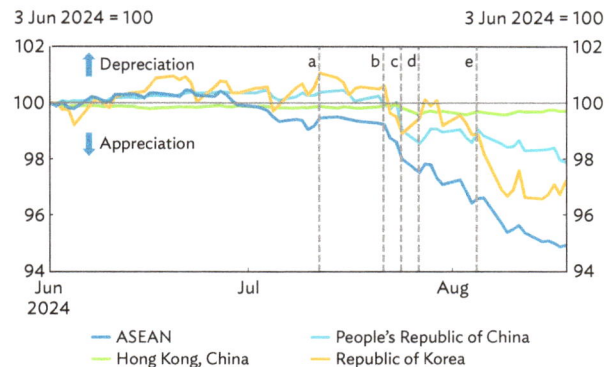

ASEAN = Association of Southeast Asian Nations.
a   Some Federal Reserve officials affirm that the timing of a policy rate cut draws near.
b   Federal Reserve Chair Jerome Powell indicates at the Federal Open Market Committee meeting that a rate cut is possible in September.
c   Market overreaction to the release of weak United States' labor market indicators and concerns of a recession.
d   Some Federal Reserve officials sought to calm financial markets.
e   More Federal Reserve officials indicated support for a policy rate cut on the release of slowing July inflation.
Notes:
1.   ASEAN comprises the markets of Indonesia, Malaysia, the Philippines, Singapore, Thailand, and Viet Nam.
2.   Data are as of 30 August 2024.
3.   A higher level indicates currency depreciation against the United States dollar.
Source: *AsianBondsOnline* calculations based on Bloomberg LP data.

cuts. For example, Bank Indonesia indicated on 8 July that a cut in the fourth quarter was possible should the rupiah continue to stabilize. Similarly, on 3 September, the Bank of Korea said that it was now time to consider cutting rates.

Regional economies demonstrated solid growth prospects during the review period. Most regional economies— particularly Hong Kong, China; Malaysia; the Philippines; Thailand; and Viet Nam—witnessed improvements in their Q2 2024 GDP performance compared to the first quarter (**Table C**). In the July edition of the *Asian Development Outlook*, the Asian Development Bank's 2024 growth projection for East Asia was revised slightly upward to 4.6% from the 4.5% forecast made in April, due to strong exports of semiconductors and artificial intelligence products from high-income economies in the region, including the Republic of Korea. The growth forecast for Southeast Asia was maintained at 4.6%, supported by strong domestic and external demand.

Expectations of rate cuts in the US supported the appreciation of emerging East Asian currencies against the US dollar during the review period. Regional currencies strengthened by 3.3% (simple average) and 2.7% (GDP-weighted average) against the US dollar during the review period. Most of the gains were observed starting in July, when the Federal Reserve hinted that a rate cut was likely in September (**Figure C**). In June, regional currencies weakened by a marginal 0.3% (both simple and GDP-weighted averages) against the US dollar due to uncertainties regarding the direction of US monetary policy, which kept the interest differential between the US dollar and local currencies relatively high. In July, the

region's currencies gained 1.0% (simple average) and 0.7% (GDP-weighted) on hints of a possible rate cut in September by the Federal Reserve. Regional currencies continued to appreciate against the US dollar in August (2.7% simple average and 2.4% GDP-weighted average) as the market expectation of a September US rate cut gained more ground. During the entire review period, the Malaysian ringgit witnessed the largest appreciation versus the US dollar (8.9%), driven by strong capital inflows and positive sentiment over the planned implementation of a consumption tax that is expected to bolster government finances. The Thai baht recorded the region's next largest appreciation at 8.6%, buoyed by increased tourist arrivals and an upgrade in the government's 2024 GDP forecast to 2.7% from a previous forecast of 2.4%.

Risk premiums narrowed in all regional markets during the review period. Risk premiums, as measured by the credit default swap (CDS) spread, narrowed by a simple average of 7.4 bps and a GDP-weighted average of 5.2 bps across emerging East Asia during the review period. This was largely driven by the expected ending of monetary tightening worldwide. In June, most regional markets' risk premiums widened on uncertainty regarding US monetary

Figure D: Changes in Credit Default Swap Spreads in Select Emerging East Asian Markets (senior 5-year)

Basis points

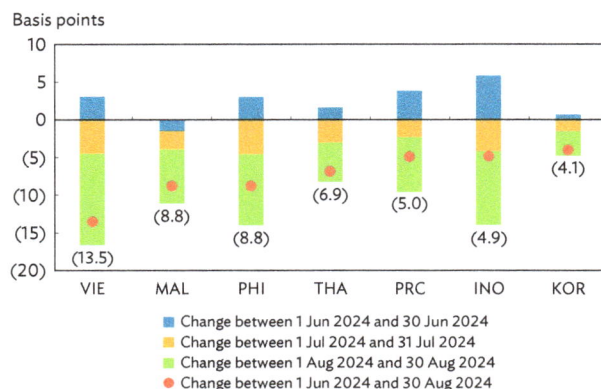

Legend:
- ■ Change between 1 Jun 2024 and 30 Jun 2024
- ■ Change between 1 Jul 2024 and 31 Jul 2024
- ■ Change between 1 Aug 2024 and 30 Aug 2024
- ● Change between 1 Jun 2024 and 30 Aug 2024

( ) = negative; INO = Indonesia; KOR = Republic of Korea; MAL = Malaysia; PHI = Philippines; PRC = People's Republic of China; THA = Thailand; VIE = Viet Nam.

Note: The numbers above (below) each bar refer to the change in spreads between 1 June 2024 and 30 August 2024.

Source: *AsianBondsOnline* calculations based on Bloomberg LP data.

Figure F: Changes in Equity Indexes in Select Emerging East Asian Markets

%

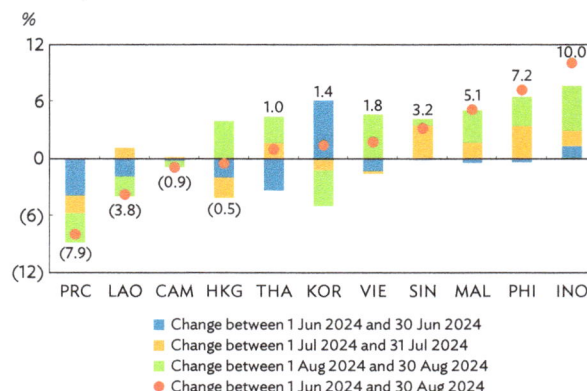

Legend:
- ■ Change between 1 Jun 2024 and 30 Jun 2024
- ■ Change between 1 Jul 2024 and 31 Jul 2024
- ■ Change between 1 Aug 2024 and 30 Aug 2024
- ● Change between 1 Jun 2024 and 30 Aug 2024

( ) = negative; CAM = Cambodia; HKG = Hong Kong, China; INO = Indonesia; KOR = Republic of Korea; LAO = Lao People's Democratic Republic; MAL = Malaysia; PHI = Philippines; PRC = People's Republic of China; SIN = Singapore; THA = Thailand; VIE = Viet Nam.

Note: The numbers above (below) each bar refer to the change between 1 June 2024 and 30 August 2024.

Source: *AsianBondsOnline* calculations based on Bloomberg LP data.

Figure E: Chicago Board Options Exchange Volatility Index

Index

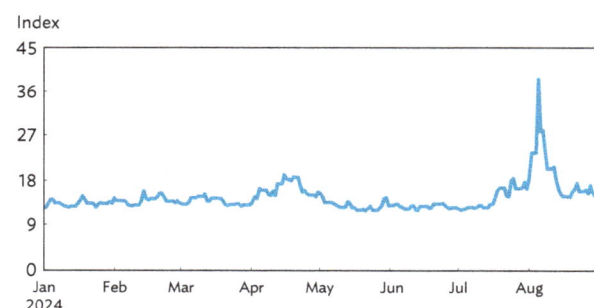

Note: Data are as of 30 August 2024.
Source: Bloomberg LP.

policy and the prospect of higher-for-longer rates. Since July, the regional CDS spread collectively narrowed as the Federal Reserve indicated it was increasingly confident that inflation was trending downward (**Figure D**). In early August, risk aversion heightened after US labor market data were released. Global risk aversion also rose over concerns of a possible recession in the US, pushing the Chicago Board Options Exchange's Volatility Index up from 16.4 to 38.6 from 31 July to 5 August (**Figure E**). After Federal Reserve officials, such as Mary Daly and Austan Goolsbee, helped to calm markets on 5 August, the volatility index subsequently recovered to 15.0 on 30 August, and risk premiums in regional markets also receded.

Most regional equity markets gained during the review period, except for the PRC and Hong Kong, China (**Figure F**). Regional equity markets recorded a market-weighted average return of −3.7% during the review period, but a market-weighted gain of 3.6% when excluding the PRC and Hong Kong, China. The weak equity performance in the PRC and Hong Kong, China was driven by continued weakness in the PRC's economy. Similar to risk premiums, most regional equity markets recorded losses in June and gains since July. Regional equity markets collectively fell from 1 August to 5 August due to heightened risk aversion on weak US labor market data (**Figure G**). However, markets subsequently recovered. Among regional markets, Indonesia and the Philippines recorded the largest gains. In Indonesia, gains were fueled by rising expectations of a policy rate cut and increased capital inflows. In the Philippines, the Bangko Sentral ng Pilipinas reduced its policy rate in August and the economy posted the region's second-highest GDP growth in Q2 2024.

Portfolio inflows were observed in regional equity and bond markets during the review period. The region recorded cumulative equity inflows of USD7.6 billion from 1 June to 30 August (**Figure H**). In June, regional equity markets recorded net portfolio outflows of USD2.1 billion over heightened uncertainty regarding US monetary policy. Beginning in July, sentiments turned positive as the Federal Reserve became confident that the inflation

Figure G: Movements in Equity Indexes in Select Emerging East Asian Markets

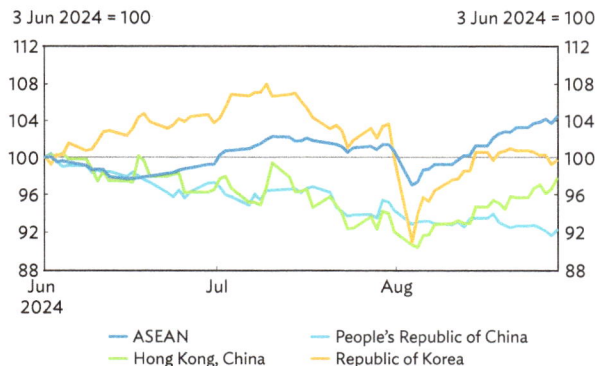

ASEAN = Association of Southeast Asian Nations.

Notes:
1. ASEAN comprises the markets of Cambodia, Indonesia, Lao People's Democratic Republic, Malaysia, the Philippines, Singapore, Thailand, and Viet Nam.
2. Data are as of 30 August 2024.

Source: *AsianBondsOnline* calculations based on Bloomberg LP data.

Figure H: Foreign Capital Flows in Select Emerging East Asian Equity Markets

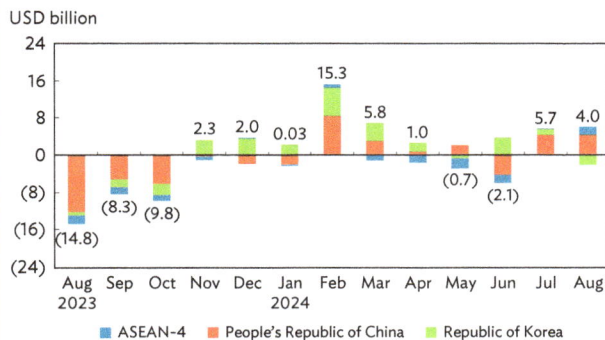

( ) = outflows, USD = United States dollar.

Notes:
1. Data coverage is from 1 August 2023 to 30 August 2024.
2. The numbers above (below) each bar refer to net inflows (net outflows) for each month.
3. Emerging East Asia is defined to include member states of the Association of Southeast Asian Nations (ASEAN) plus the People's Republic of China; Hong Kong, China; and the Republic of Korea.
4. ASEAN-4 includes Indonesia, the Philippines, Thailand, and Viet Nam.

Source: Institute of International Finance.

Figure I: Foreign Capital Flows in Select Emerging East Asian Local Currency Bond Markets

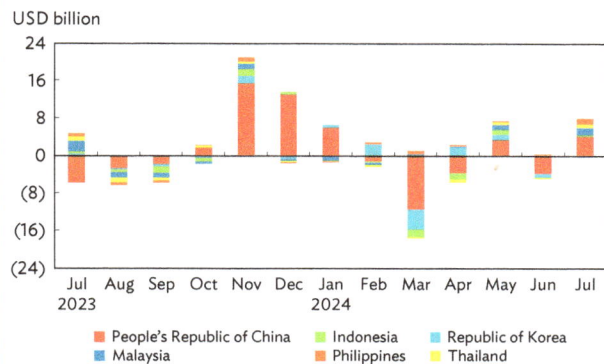

( ) = negative, USD = United States dollar.

Notes:
1. The Republic of Korea and Thailand provided data on bond flows. For the People's Republic of China, Indonesia, Malaysia, and the Philippines, month-on-month changes in foreign holdings of local currency government bonds were used as a proxy for bond flows.
2. Data are as of 31 July 2024.
3. Figures were computed based on 31 July 2024 exchange rates and do not include currency effects.

Sources: People's Republic of China (Bloomberg LP); Indonesia (Directorate General of Budget Financing and Risk Management, Ministry of Finance); Republic of Korea (Financial Supervisory Service); Malaysia (Bank Negara Malaysia); Philippines (Bureau of the Treasury); and Thailand (Thai Bond Market Association).

The risk outlook to regional financial conditions remains balanced. On the upside, the regional economy is strong. Regional price pressures continued to gradually ease due to a slight decrease in global food prices and the lagged effect of tight monetary policy, despite ongoing oil price volatility. Additionally, the anticipated rate cuts in the US may allow many central banks in the region to cut rates during the second half of the year. Expected rate cuts by central banks, both within the region and in advanced economies, are projected to support financial conditions and bolster investor confidence. **Box 1** discusses how macroeconomic factors affect the resilience of emerging markets to changes in US monetary policy cycles.

Despite a still sound regional economy and moderating inflation, several downside factors could undermine these positive trends. First, ongoing trade tensions between the US and the PRC could disrupt global supply chains and weigh upon the region's trade and economic performance. Uncertainty surrounding the US election's outcome, which could potentially lead to broader US tariffs on a wider range of Chinese imports, contributes to the uncertainty surrounding trade tensions. Rising trade tensions may exacerbate market volatility, lead to capital outflows, strain regional currencies, and affect financial stability. Second, the PRC's weaker-than-expected

path supported a rate cut. Between 1 July and 30 August, the region recorded inflows of USD9.7 billion. Similar to the region's equity markets, bond market sentiment also improved in July when inflows of USD7.7 billion were recorded in the region's bond markets. In June, capital outflows of USD4.6 billion were recorded in regional bond markets, much of which came from the PRC's bond market on concerns over its growth outlook and property sector (**Figure I**).

economic performance could have spillover effects across the region, as declining consumer and investor sentiment in the PRC would reduce demand for regional goods and services, and increase risk aversion in financial markets. Third, escalating geopolitical tensions pose risks to oil prices. Wider conflict in the Middle East might further disrupt shipping routes and push up oil and commodity prices, which could reignite inflationary pressures. In addition, domestic uncertainties in some ASEAN economies could raise investor risk aversion and weaken financial conditions in the region. For instance, in Thailand, the prime minister was dismissed following a court ruling on 14 August. Lastly, adverse weather conditions and the impacts of climate change pose risks to food and energy security, and contribute to supply chain disruptions, potentially leading to persistent inflation. This, in turn, would affect central bank decisions regarding interest rates, and thus impact global and regional financial conditions. The outlook to regional financial conditions is also exposed to market volatility in response to negative news, similar to what was observed in early August.

Box 1: Why Are Some Emerging Markets More Resilient to United States Monetary Policy Cycles Than Others?

The United States (US) dollar continues to reign supreme. The dollar dominates international trade and financial transactions, and the foreign exchange reserves of central banks. As such, US monetary policy still drives global financial cycles, impacting global capital flows and credit growth. Dollar dominance ultimately limits the policy choices of financially integrated emerging markets.

The global influence of US monetary policy was especially visible during the 7 years of easing (2007–2014) induced by the global financial crisis and its aftermath. This was followed by 4.5 years of tightening that was kicked off by the 2013 "taper tantrum." Subsequently, 3 years of easing (2019–2022), largely induced by the COVID-19 pandemic, eventually led to a major tightening beginning in February 2022 as a delayed reaction to rapidly rising inflation in the US (**Figure B1**).

As US monetary policy shifts have global repercussions, capital markets in emerging economies are often vulnerable to destabilizing flight-to-quality outflows during periods of heightened uncertainty. They are also vulnerable to volatile

Figure B1: Monetary Cycles in the United States

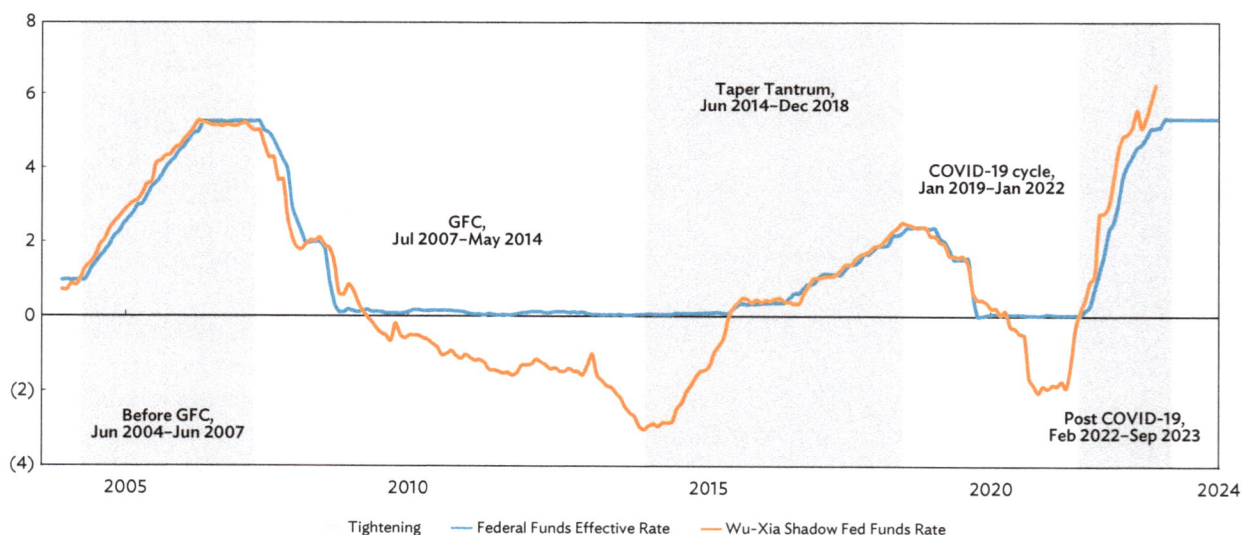

COVID-19 = coronavirus disease, GFC = global financial crisis.
Sources: Atlanta Federal Reserve Bank. Wu–Xia Shadow Federal Funds Rate; St. Louis Federal Reserve Bank. Federal Funds.

This box was written by Donghyun Park (economic advisor) and Irfan Qureshi (public management specialist) of the Asian Development Bank.

continued on next page

Box 1 *continued*

search-for-yield inflows during periods of low returns in the US. Large inflows were observed when the Federal Reserve's massive monetary easing pushed the federal funds rate close to zero in the wake of the global financial crisis.

At a broader level, these episodes placed increasing pressure on the macroeconomic outlook of emerging markets and raised their risk profile. They also impacted emerging market currencies, debt repayments, and capital flows. For instance, 2023 saw many currencies in developing Asia depreciate substantially versus the US dollar due to aggressive tightening by the Federal Reserve (Asian Development Bank 2023).

A natural question that arises is why some emerging markets are more resilient and/or less vulnerable to US monetary policy cycles, an issue examined by Aizenman et al. (2024). They sought to empirically assess whether macroeconomic variables such as debt level and institutional variables such as degree of corruption can explain an emerging market's resilience during each cycle. The three measures of emerging market resilience included in this study are (i) the bilateral exchange rate against the US dollar, (ii) exchange rate market pressure, and (iii) the market-specific Morgan Stanley Capital International Index. In addition, the role of policy factors such as exchange rate regime type and inflation targeting were also examined.

At the broadest level, the existing research finds that macroeconomic and institutional variables are indeed significantly associated with emerging market performance. Furthermore, the determinants of resilience differ during tightening versus easing cycles, and the quality of institutions matters even more during difficult times.

The findings of Aizenman et al. (2024) can be succinctly described as follows. First and foremost, cross-market differences in ex-ante macroeconomic fundamentals and institutional variables can help explain the differences in performance and resilience of a large cross-section of emerging markets during different US monetary cycles. Second, these determinants differ during tightening versus easing cycles. Third, the significance of ex-ante institutional variables increased during the monetary cycles triggered by the global financial crisis and the taper tantrum. This suggests that good institutions matter more during difficult times.

Finally, emerging market policymakers can draw some policy implications from the paper's empirical findings. For instance, the authors find that international reserves, the current account balance, and inflation are all important determinants of an emerging market's resilience to US monetary policy swings. This reinforces the conventional wisdom that strong fundamentals protect emerging markets in the face of large external shocks.

References

J. Aizenman, D. Park, I.A. Qureshi, G.S. Uddin, and J. Saadaoui. 2024. The Performance of Emerging Markets During the Fed's Easing and Tightening Cycles: A Cross-Country Resilience Analysis. *Journal of International Money and Finance.*

Asian Development Bank. 2023. *Asian Development Outlook.* Manila.

L.S. Goldberg and S. Krogstrup. 2023. International Capital Flow Pressures and Global Factors. *National Bureau of Economic Research Working Paper No. 30887.*

Bond Market Developments in the Second Quarter of 2024

Section 1. Local Currency Bonds Outstanding

Emerging East Asian local currency (LCY) bonds outstanding rose to USD25.1 trillion at the end of June on a year-on-year (y-o-y) expansion of 9.2%.[2] The pace of annual growth in the emerging East Asian LCY bond market continued to surpass that of the United States (US) (6.8%) and the European Union 20 (EU-20) (5.0%). At the end of June, the size of the emerging East Asian LCY bond market was equivalent to 64.7% of the US market (USD38.7 trillion) and 115.8% of the EU-20 market (USD21.6 trillion) (**Figure 1**).

Figure 1: Local Currency Bonds Outstanding in Emerging East Asia, the European Union 20, and the United States

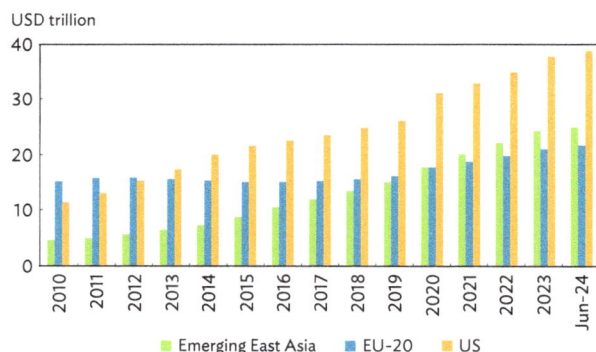

USD trillion

Legend: Emerging East Asia, EU-20, US

EU-20 = European Union 20, US = United States, USD = United States dollar.

Notes:
1. Emerging East Asia is defined to include the Association of Southeast Asian Nations plus the People's Republic of China; Hong Kong, China; and the Republic of Korea.
2. The EU-20 includes the member markets of Austria, Belgium, Croatia, Cyprus, Estonia, Finland, France, Germany, Greece, Ireland, Italy, Latvia, Lithuania, Luxembourg, Malta, the Netherlands, Portugal, Slovakia, Slovenia, and Spain.

Sources: People's Republic of China (CEIC Data Company); Hong Kong, China (Hong Kong Monetary Authority); EU-20 (European Central Bank); Indonesia (Bank Indonesia; Directorate General of Budget Financing and Risk Management, Ministry of Finance; and Indonesia Stock Exchange); Republic of Korea (Bank of Korea and KG Zeroin Corporation); Malaysia (Bank Negara Malaysia); Philippines (Bureau of the Treasury and Bloomberg LP); Singapore (Monetary Authority of Singapore and Bloomberg LP); Thailand (Bank of Thailand); United States (Securities Industry and Financial Markets Association and Bloomberg LP); and Viet Nam (Vietnam Bond Market Association and Bloomberg LP).

Increased issuance of Treasury bonds in the People's Republic of China (PRC) helped offset slower growth in the rest of emerging East Asia. Total LCY bonds outstanding grew 2.3% quarter-on-quarter (q-o-q) in the second quarter (Q2) of 2024, up from 1.4% q-o-q in the first quarter (Q1) (**Table 1**). The stock of corporate bonds grew 1.5% q-o-q in Q2 2024, up from 1.2% in Q1 2024, due to increased issuance in the PRC and most members of the Association of Southeast Asian Nations (ASEAN). To finance stimulus measures to support the slowing economy, the Government of the PRC increased Treasury bond issuance by 41.6% q-o-q in Q2 2024 (**Figure 2**). Five of the region's nine LCY bond markets saw slower growth in Q2 2024 than in the previous quarter (**Figure 3**), with actual contractions in Hong Kong, China (as Treasury bonds matured); Thailand (as issuance of central bank bonds fell); and Viet Nam (as issuance of both central bank and Treasury bonds declined). In Hong Kong, China, issuance of government bonds contracted amid a transition from the existing government bond program to the newly established infrastructure and sustainable bond programs. Central bank issuance in Thailand, as well as government and central bank issuance in Viet Nam, declined in response to domestic market liquidity conditions.

The share of ASEAN members' outstanding bonds in emerging East Asia's overall LCY bond market remained below 10%. At the end of June, the aggregate amount of ASEAN LCY bonds outstanding reached USD2.2 trillion, comprising 8.9% of the emerging East Asian LCY bond market (**Figure 4**). Within ASEAN, Singapore's LCY bond market (USD0.6 trillion) was the largest and Viet Nam's market (USD0.1 trillion) remained the smallest. Meanwhile, the PRC's LCY bond market (USD20.0 trillion) represented 79.7% of the emerging East Asian total, while that of the Republic of Korea (USD2.5 trillion) and Hong Kong, China (USD0.4 trillion) accounted for 9.9% and 1.6% shares, respectively. Treasury bonds (USD15.6 trillion) remained the dominant type of LCY bond in emerging East Asia, representing 62.3% of the region's total outstanding bonds; corporate

---

[2] Emerging East Asia is defined to include member states of the Association of Southeast Asian Nations plus the People's Republic of China; Hong Kong, China; and the Republic of Korea.

Table 1: Size and Composition of Select Emerging East Asian Local Currency Bond Markets

	Q2 2023		Q1 2024		Q2 2024			Growth Rate (%) Q2 2024	
	Amount (USD billion)	% of GDP	Amount (USD billion)	% of GDP	Amount (USD billion)	% share	% of GDP	q-o-q	y-o-y
People's Republic of China									
Total	18,325	107.6	19,667	111.6	19,971	100.0	113.0	2.2	9.2
Treasury and Other Government	12,122	71.2	13,031	74.0	13,320	66.7	75.3	2.8	10.1
Central Bank	2	0.01	2	0.01	2	0.01	0.01	0.0	0.0
Corporate	6,201	36.4	6,634	37.7	6,649	33.3	37.6	0.9	7.4
Hong Kong, China									
Total	367	100.1	389	100.5	389	100.0	98.4	(0.4)	5.5
Treasury and Other Government	30	8.2	37	9.5	33	8.5	8.4	(9.9)	10.4
Government	157	42.7	162	41.9	164	42.2	41.6	1.0	4.4
Corporate	181	49.3	190	49.2	191	49.2	48.4	0.2	5.6
Indonesia									
Total	409	29.9	428	32.1	440	100.0	33.6	6.1	17.4
Treasury and Other Government	376	27.5	370	27.8	364	82.9	27.9	1.6	5.9
Central Bank	4	0.3	29	2.2	47	10.7	3.6	69	1,334.3
Corporate	30	2.2	29	2.2	28	6.4	2.2	1.1	4.5
Republic of Korea									
Total	2,347	131.8	2,426	133.9	2,469	100.0	136.8	3.9	9.9
Treasury and Other Government	904	50.8	906	50.0	911	36.9	50.4	2.7	5.2
Central Bank	94	5.3	89	4.9	87	3.5	2.1	(0.3)	(3.7)
Corporate	1,349	75.8	1,431	79.0	1,471	59.6	81.5	5.0	14.0
Malaysia									
Total	419	126.5	432	128.8	437	100.0	128.2	0.9	5.5
Treasury and Other Government	239	72.2	250	74.4	254	58.2	74.6	1.6	7.5
Central Bank	3	0.8	3	0.8	0.4	0.1	0.1	(84.6)	(83.3)
Corporate	177	53.5	180	53.6	182	41.7	53.5	1.3	4.0
Philippines									
Total	212	50.4	219	49.5	214	100.0	49.3	1.9	7.1
Treasury and Other Government	175	41.5	180	40.9	178	83.3	41.0	2.8	8.2
Central Bank	8	2.0	14	3.1	14	6.5	3.2	6.8	74.4
Corporate	29	6.9	25	5.6	22	10.2	5.0	(7.7)	(19.4)
Singapore									
Total	503	100.9	545	107.3	572	100.0	111.0	5.5	14.1
Treasury and Other Government	180	36.1	192	37.9	205	35.9	39.9	7.2	14.6
Central Bank	198	39.7	228	44.9	238	41.6	46.1	4.7	20.6
Corporate	125	25.2	124	24.4	129	22.5	25.0	4.3	3.1
Thailand									
Total	459	91.7	465	94.0	460	100.0	92.8	(0.2)	3.9
Treasury and Other Government	257	51.4	269	54.2	269	58.5	54.3	1.1	8.4
Central Bank	67	13.4	65	13.1	61	13.2	12.3	(5.3)	(5.9)
Corporate	135	26.9	132	26.6	130	28.3	26.3	(0.4)	0.3
Viet Nam									
Total	108	25.9	116	27.5	108	100.0	25.8	(3.7)	8.5
Treasury and Other Government	79	18.9	81	19.3	81	74.5	19.2	2.2	10.8
Central Bank	0	0.0	6	1.4	0	0.0	0.0	(100.0)	–
Corporate	29	7.0	29	6.8	28	25.5	6.6	(0.8)	2.2
Emerging East Asia									
Total	23,147	101.9	24,687	105.7	25,059	100.0	107.1	2.3	9.2
Treasury and Other Government	14,360	63.2	15,317	65.6	15,615	62.3	66.8	2.8	9.7
Central Bank	532	2.3	597	2.6	613	2.4	2.6	3.5	16.7
Corporate	8,255	36.4	8,773	37.6	8,831	35.2	37.8	1.5	8.0
Japan									
Total	9,358	234.2	9,078	230.4	8,559	100.0	229.7	0.2	2.0
Treasury and Other Government	8,654	216.6	8,376	212.5	7,889	92.2	211.7	0.1	1.6
Central Bank	14	0.3	25	0.6	23	0.3	0.6	(2.4)	82.3
Corporate	691	17.3	677	17.2	647	7.6	17.4	1.60	4.4

( ) = negative, – = not applicable, GDP = gross domestic product, q-o-q = quarter-on-quarter, Q1 = first quarter, Q2 = second quarter, USD = United States dollar, y-o-y = year-on-year.

Notes:
1. For Singapore, corporate bonds outstanding are based on *AsianBondsOnline* estimates.
2. GDP data are from CEIC Data Company.
3. Bloomberg LP end-of-period local currency–USD rates are used.
4. Growth rates are calculated from a local currency base and do not include currency effects. For emerging East Asia, growth figures are based on 30 June 2024 currency exchange rates and do not include currency effects.

Sources: People's Republic of China (CEIC Data Company); Hong Kong, China (Hong Kong Monetary Authority); Indonesia (Bank Indonesia; Directorate General of Budget Financing and Risk Management, Ministry of Finance; and Indonesia Stock Exchange); Japan (Japan Securities Dealers Association); Republic of Korea (Bank of Korea and KG Zeroin Corporation); Malaysia (Bank Negara Malaysia); Philippines (Bureau of the Treasury and Bloomberg LP); Singapore (Monetary Authority of Singapore and Bloomberg LP); Thailand (Bank of Thailand); and Viet Nam (Vietnam Bond Market Association and Bloomberg LP).

Figure 2: Real Gross Domestic Product Growth in the People's Republic of China (y-o-y, %)

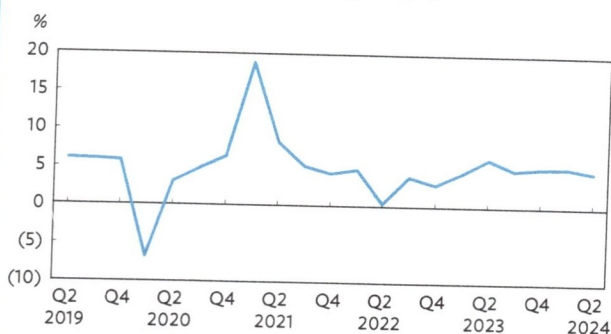

( ) = negative, Q2 = second quarter, Q4 = fourth quarter, y-o-y = year-on-year.
Source: National Bureau of Statistics of China.

Figure 3: Growth of Select Emerging East Asian Local Currency Bond Markets (q-o-q, %)

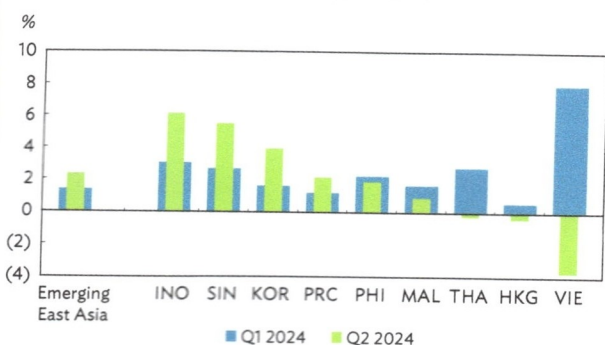

■ Q1 2024   ■ Q2 2024

( ) = negative; HKG = Hong Kong, China; INO = Indonesia; KOR = Republic of Korea; MAL = Malaysia; PHI = Philippines; PRC = People's Republic of China; Q1 = first quarter; Q2 = second quarter; q-o-q = quarter-on-quarter; SIN = Singapore; THA = Thailand; VIE = Viet Nam.

Notes:
1. For Singapore, corporate bonds outstanding are based on *AsianBondsOnline* estimates.
2. Growth rates are calculated from a local currency base and do not include currency effects. For emerging East Asia, growth figures are based on 30 June 2024 currency exchange rates and do not include currency effects.
3. Emerging East Asia is defined to include member states of the Association of Southeast Asian Nations plus the People's Republic of China; Hong Kong, China; and the Republic of Korea.

Sources: People's Republic of China (CEIC Data Company); Hong Kong, China (Hong Kong Monetary Authority); Indonesia (Bank Indonesia; Directorate General of Budget Financing and Risk Management, Ministry of Finance; and Indonesia Stock Exchange); Republic of Korea (Bank of Korea and KG Zeroin Corporation); Malaysia (Bank Negara Malaysia); Philippines (Bureau of the Treasury and Bloomberg LP); Singapore (Monetary Authority of Singapore and Bloomberg LP); Thailand (Bank of Thailand); and Viet Nam (Vietnam Bond Market Association and Bloomberg LP).

Figure 4: Local Currency Bonds Outstanding in Emerging East Asia by Economy and Type of Bond as of 30 June 2024

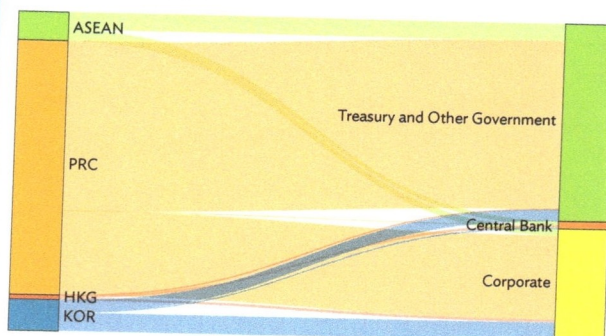

ASEAN = Association of Southeast Asian Nations; HKG = Hong Kong, China; KOR = Republic of Korea; PRC = People's Republic of China.
Note: ASEAN comprises the markets of Indonesia, Malaysia, the Philippines, Singapore, Thailand, and Viet Nam.
Source: *AsianBondsOnline* calculations based on various local sources.

bonds (USD8.8 trillion) and central bank bonds (USD0.6 trillion) comprised 35.2% and 2.4% shares, respectively.

Treasury bonds in ASEAN markets remained concentrated mainly in medium- to long-term maturities. At the end of June, 60.2% of Treasury bonds outstanding in ASEAN markets had remaining maturities of over 5 years (**Figure 5**). The corresponding share for emerging East Asia was slightly lower at 52.6%. The size-weighted average tenor of emerging East Asian Treasury bonds outstanding was 8.6 years at the end of June. ASEAN's size-weighted average tenor was 8.1 years, broadly comparable with the average of 8.8 years for the rest of the region (i.e., the PRC; Hong Kong, China; and the Republic of Korea). These averages are largely in line with the corresponding size-weighted average tenors of outstanding Treasury bonds in the EU-20 (8.4 years) and the US (8.0 years) during the same period. With the issuance of Treasury bonds with 20-, 30-, and 50-year maturities in the PRC in Q2 2024, the size-weighted average tenor of the PRC's Treasury bonds inched up to 8.2 years at the end of June from 7.4 years at the end of March. The ultra-long-term bond issuances from the PRC aim to ease the financing burden on local governments.

Figure 5: Maturity Structure of Local Currency Treasury Bonds Outstanding in Select Emerging East Asian Markets as of 30 June 2024

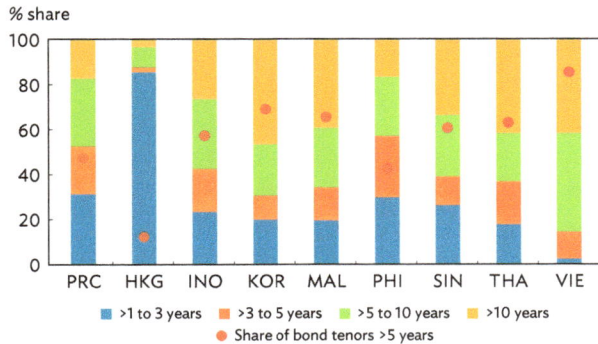

HKG = Hong Kong, China; INO = Indonesia; KOR = Republic of Korea; MAL = Malaysia; PHI = Philippines; PRC = People's Republic of China; SIN = Singapore; THA = Thailand; VIE = Viet Nam.

Note: Treasury bonds are local-currency-denominated, fixed-income securities issued by a government with maturities longer than 1 year.

Sources: People's Republic of China (Bloomberg LP); Hong Kong, China (Hong Kong Monetary Authority); Indonesia (Directorate General of Budget Financing and Risk Management, Ministry of Finance); Republic of Korea (Bloomberg LP); Malaysia (Bank Negara Malaysia Fully Automated System for Issuing/Tendering); Philippines (Bureau of the Treasury); Singapore (Monetary Authority of Singapore); Thailand (Bank of Thailand); and Viet Nam (Bloomberg LP).

LCY Treasury bonds in emerging East Asia remained dominated by inactive domestic investor groups, which tend to buy and hold securities until maturity. Banks and insurance companies comprised the largest investor groups in emerging East Asia in the first half of 2024, accounting for average holdings shares of 36.2% and 28.9%, respectively. Across the region, banking institutions were the largest holders of Treasury bonds in the PRC (70.4%), while insurance and pension funds were the dominant holders in Viet Nam (60.8%) (**Figure 6**). The high concentration of bond holdings in these investor groups led the PRC and Viet Nam to have the least diversified investor profiles in the region, as evidenced by their high scores in the Herfindahl–Hirschman Index (HHI).[3] Both markets also recorded a worsening in their respective HHI scores in the first half of the 2024. In the case of the PRC, the weakened economic outlook led to continued outflows from foreign investors. In Viet Nam's bond market, banks and insurance and pension funds are the only two major investor groups, collectively accounting for a 99.5% holdings share at the end of March. In contrast, Indonesia and the Republic of Korea have the most diversified investor bases in emerging

Figure 6: Investor Profiles of Local Currency Treasury Bonds in Select Emerging East Asian Markets

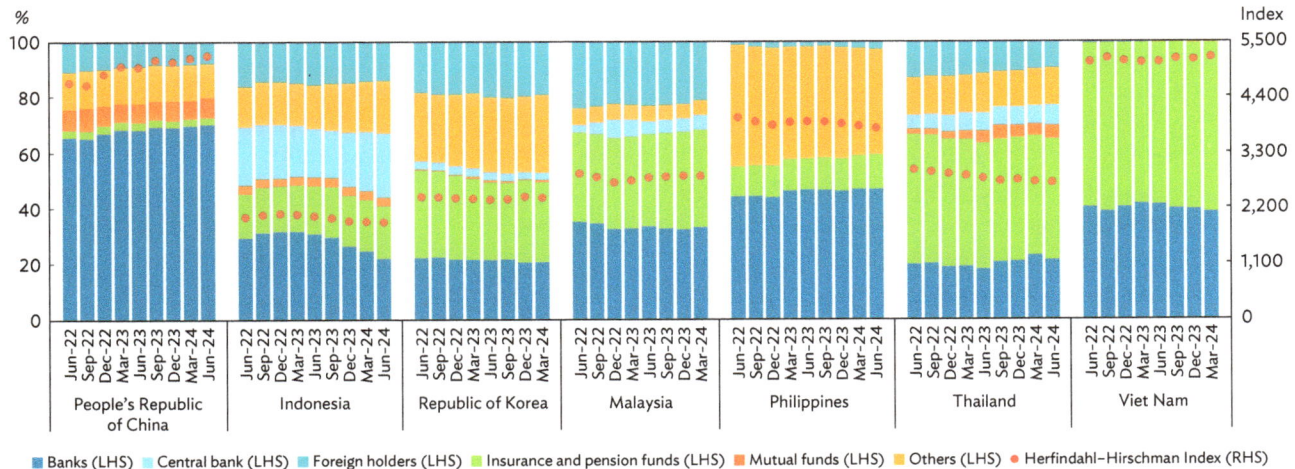

LHS = left-hand side, RHS = right-hand side.
Notes:
1. Data for the Republic of Korea, Malaysia, and Viet Nam are up to March 2024.
2. "Others" include government institutions, individuals, securities companies, custodians, private corporations, and all other investors not elsewhere classified.
3. The Herfindahl–Hirschman Index is a commonly accepted measure of market concentration. In this case, the index was used to measure the investor profile diversification of the local currency bond markets and is calculated by summing the squared share of each investor group in the bond market.

Sources: People's Republic of China (CEIC Data Company); Indonesia (Directorate General of Budget Financing and Risk Management, Ministry of Finance); Republic of Korea (Bank of Korea); Malaysia (Bank Negara Malaysia); Philippines (Bureau of the Treasury); Thailand (Bank of Thailand); and Viet Nam (Ministry of Finance).

---

[3] HHI is a commonly accepted measure of market concentration. The index is used to measure the investor profile diversification of the region's local currency bond markets and is calculated by summing the squared share of each investor group in the bond market.

East Asia. Among regional bond markets, only the central bank in Indonesia has substantial holdings of bonds, accounting for a share of 23.1% at the end of June, as Bank Indonesia continues to actively support the LCY bond market, particularly during market sell-offs. Meanwhile, the region's average holdings share of foreign investors for Treasury bonds stood at 10.6% in the first half of 2024. Malaysia had the largest foreign holdings share for Treasury bonds at 21.2%, followed by the Republic of Korea at 19.2%.

Section 2. Local Currency Bond Issuance

LCY bond issuance in emerging East Asia rebounded in Q2 2024, posting growth of 15.4% q-o-q, a reversal from the 9.1% q-o-q contraction in Q1 2024; bond market growth was driven by expansions in both the government and corporate bond segments. Total LCY bond issuance reached USD2.6 trillion in Q2 2024, over half the issuance total in the US (USD4.5 trillion) and more than double that in the EU-20 (USD0.9 trillion). Growth in Q2 2024 largely stemmed from the government bond segment, driven by a surge in issuance in the PRC as the government ramped up its fiscal policy to support the economy. This included continued high issuance volumes for local government bonds during the quarter and the start of the sale of ultra-long-term special Treasury bonds in May. Regional corporate bond issuance also rose in Q2 2024, albeit at a slower pace, led by the PRC and most ASEAN economies (**Figure 7**). Issuance in the PRC increased in Q2 2024, driven by increased issuance of financial bonds as banks raised funds to meet regulatory capital requirements. Most ASEAN markets also posted larger quarterly corporate bond issuance volumes due to bond yields being driven lower by the Federal Reserve's expected rate cut.

Government bond issuance surged 27.0% q-o-q to USD1.1 trillion in Q2 2024, driven by increased issuance in the PRC. Issuance in the PRC, which remained the largest issuer of government bonds in the region in Q2 2024 with an 85.9% share, jumped 32.2% q-o-q as all types of government bonds registered quarterly increases (**Figure 8**). Treasury bonds rose 41.6% q-o-q, boosted by the sale of the first few batches of ultra-long-term special Treasury bonds. In March, the Government of the PRC announced its plan to issue CNY1.0 trillion worth of ultra-long-term special Treasury bonds from May to

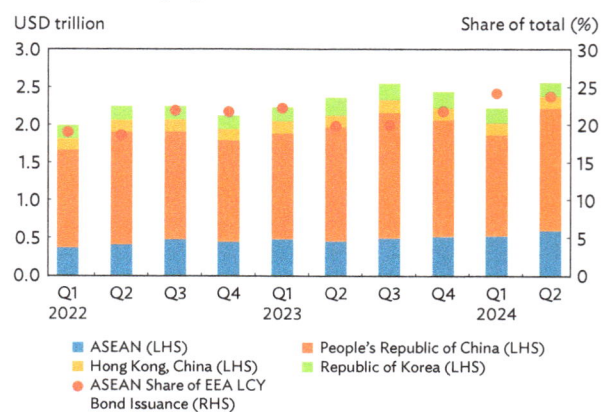

Figure 7: Local Currency Bond Issuance in Select Emerging East Asian Markets

ASEAN = Association of Southeast Asian Nations, EEA = emerging East Asia, LCY = local currency, LHS = left-hand side, Q1 = first quarter, Q2 = second quarter, Q3 = third quarter, Q4 = fourth quarter, RHS = right-hand side, USD = United States dollar.
Notes:
1. ASEAN comprises the markets of Indonesia, Malaysia, the Philippines, Singapore, Thailand, and Viet Nam.
2. Figures were computed based on 30 June 2024 currency exchange rates and do not include currency effects.
Source: People's Republic of China (CEIC Data Company); Hong Kong, China (Hong Kong Monetary Authority); Indonesia (Bank Indonesia; Directorate General of Budget Financing and Risk Management, Ministry of Finance; and Indonesia Stock Exchange); Republic of Korea (Bank of Korea and KG Zeroin Corporation); Malaysia (Bank Negara Malaysia); Philippines (Bureau of the Treasury and Bloomberg LP); Singapore (Monetary Authority of Singapore and Bloomberg LP); Thailand (Bank of Thailand and Thai Bond Market Association); and Viet Nam (Vietnam Bond Market Association and Bloomberg LP).

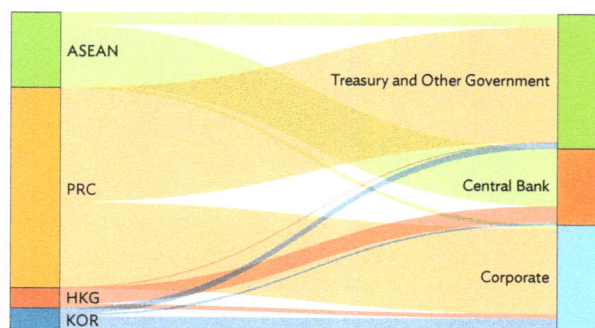

Figure 8: Local Currency Bond Issuance in Emerging East Asia by Economy and Type of Bond in the Second Quarter of 2024

ASEAN = Association of Southeast Asian Nations; HKG = Hong Kong, China; KOR = Republic of Korea; PRC = People's Republic of China.
Note: ASEAN comprises the markets of Indonesia, Malaysia, the Philippines, Singapore, Thailand, and Viet Nam.
Source: *AsianBondsOnline* calculations based on various local sources.

November to support the economy. Local government bond and policy bank bond issuance also posted large increases of 26.7% q-o-q and 21.9% q-o-q, respectively, in Q2 2024. The Republic of Korea posted a quarterly increase of 15.4% q-o-q, in line with the government's frontloading policy during the first half of the year. ASEAN markets, which collectively accounted for about a tenth of the regional government bond market in Q2 2024, registered a 1.7% q-o-q contraction in issuance, led by the drop in the Philippines from a high base in Q1 2024 when it issued USD10.4 billion worth of Retail Treasury Bonds. Meanwhile, issuance of central bank bonds in the region rose 12.0% q-o-q in Q2 2024.

Corporate bond issuance rose in Q2 2024, driven by higher issuance in the PRC and most ASEAN markets. Corporate bond issuance in emerging East Asia totaled USD860.9 billion during the quarter, up 5.6% q-o-q (**Table 2**). In the PRC, issuance rose 9.2% q-o-q, solely driven by the 62.7% q-o-q increase in financial bonds. Issuance of financial bonds rose in Q2 2024 as banks

raised capital to comply with regulatory requirements. Issuance in ASEAN collectively rose 25.4% q-o-q as bond yields eased on increased expectations of a rate cut in the US in September. Meanwhile, in the Republic of Korea, issuance fell 13.9% q-o-q because funding needs were low, especially in the manufacturing sector, which was beset by slower domestic and global growth.

Medium- and long-term tenors continued to comprise a majority of Treasury bond issuance. Bonds with tenors of more than 5 years accounted for 55.9% of total issuance in emerging East Asia and 61.3% in ASEAN markets (**Figure 9a**). These shares were highest in the Philippines (90.0%) and Malaysia (71.1%) (**Figure 9b**). The resulting size-weighted average maturity for all emerging East Asian corporate issuance in Q2 2024 was 9.5 years; it was 11.1 years for ASEAN markets only. The average tenor of PRC Treasury bond issuance jumped to 9.5 years in Q2 2024 from 6.3 years in Q1 2024, as the government began issuing special ultra-long-term bonds with tenors of 20–50 years.

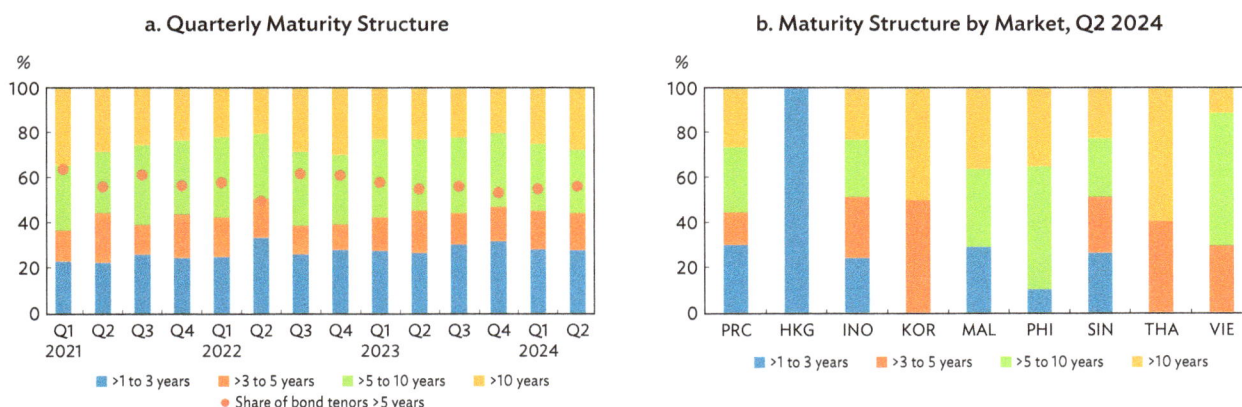

Figure 9: Maturity Structure of Local Currency Treasury Bond Issuance in Emerging East Asia

a. Quarterly Maturity Structure

b. Maturity Structure by Market, Q2 2024

HKG = Hong Kong, China; INO = Indonesia; KOR = Republic of Korea; MAL = Malaysia; PHI = Philippines; PRC = People's Republic of China; Q1 = first quarter; Q2 = second quarter; Q3 = third quarter; Q4 = fourth quarter; SIN = Singapore; THA = Thailand; VIE = Viet Nam.

Notes:
1. Figures were computed based on 30 June 2024 currency exchange rates and do not include currency effects.
2. Treasury bonds are local-currency-denominated, fixed-income securities issued by a government with maturities longer than 1 year.

Source: *AsianBondsOnline* calculations based on various local sources.

Table 2: Local-Currency-Denominated Bond Issuance

	Q2 2023		Q1 2024		Q2 2024		Growth Rate (%)	
							Q2 2024	
	Amount (USD billion)	% share	Amount (USD billion)	% share	Amount (USD billion)	% share	q-o-q	y-o-y
People's Republic of China								
Total	1,488	100.0	1,335	100.0	1,609	100.0	21.3	8.3
Treasury and Other Government	837	56.2	703	52.7	923	57.4	32.2	10.6
Central Bank	0	0.0	0	0.0	0	0.0	–	–
Corporate	651	43.8	632	47.3	686	42.6	9.2	5.4
Hong Kong, China								
Total	156	100.0	162	100.0	163	100.0	0.4	4.4
Treasury and Other Government	1	0.8	1	0.4	0.2	0.1	(72.7)	(84.2)
Government	127	81.7	128	79.1	130	79.8	1.3	2.0
Corporate	27	17.6	33	20	33	20.1	(1.3)	19.7
Indonesia								
Total	23	100.0	43	100.0	46	100.0	12.3	117.4
Treasury and Other Government	10	43.4	16	37.6	12	25.7	(23.4)	28.5
Central Bank	12	52.0	25	58.6	32	69.8	33.6	191.9
Corporate	1	4.6	2	3.8	2	4.5	35.8	114.5
Republic of Korea								
Total	237	100.0	193	100.0	176	100.0	(6.8)	(22.7)
Treasury and Other Government	55	23.2	43	22.4	49	27.8	15.4	(7.1)
Central Bank	30	12.7	18	9.3	16	9.1	(9.0)	(44.5)
Corporate	152	64.2	132	68.2	111	63.1	(13.9)	(23.9)
Malaysia								
Total	25	100.0	29	100.0	25	100.0	(13.6)	1.6
Treasury and Other Government	13	53.6	11	37.1	13	53.7	25.0	1.7
Central Bank	3	10.5	10	36.4	3	10.3	(75.5)	0.0
Corporate	9	35.9	8	26.5	9	36.0	17.1	1.8
Philippines								
Total	39	100.0	56	100.0	45	100.0	(15.7)	21.3
Treasury and Other Government	10	26.3	22	39.9	10	22.9	(51.7)	5.5
Central Bank	28	70.7	32	57.8	34	75.5	10.1	29.4
Corporate	1	3.0	1	2.3	1	1.6	(41.2)	(33.4)
Singapore								
Total	310	100.0	340	100.0	417	100.0	23.2	34.8
Treasury and Other Government	34	10.8	37	10.7	46	11.1	27.3	37.8
Central Bank	276	88.8	301	88.4	368	88.1	22.8	33.7
Corporate	1	0.4	3	0.9	3	0.8	17.7	189.7
Thailand								
Total	70	100.0	60	100.0	62	100.0	3.5	(8.7)
Treasury and Other Government	18	25.5	17	28.4	18	29.9	9.1	6.9
Central Bank	35	49.8	32	52.9	30	48.1	(5.8)	(11.7)
Corporate	17	24.7	11	18.8	14	22.0	21.1	(18.9)
Viet Nam								
Total	3	100.0	11	100.0	7	100.0	(29.4)	127.7
Treasury and Other Government	3	82.7	4	37.3	3	35.0	(33.8)	(3.6)
Central Bank	0	0.0	6	56.0	2	25.6	(67.7)	–
Corporate	1	17.3	1	6.7	3	39.5	314.5	418.4
Emerging East Asia								
Total	2,352	100.0	2,228	100.0	2,550	100.0	15.4	9.4
Treasury and Other Government	981	41.7	853	38.3	1,075	42.2	27.0	10.3
Central Bank	510	21.7	553	24.8	614	24.1	12.0	21.7
Corporate	861	36.6	822	36.9	861	33.8	5.6	1.0
Japan								
Total	380	100.0	371	100.0	330	100.0	(5.3)	(3.0)
Treasury and Other Government	349	91.9	351	94.6	296	89.8	(10.1)	(5.3)
Central Bank	0	0.0	0	0.0	0	0.0	–	–
Corporate	31	8.1	20	5.4	34	10.2	79.0	22.6

( ) = negative, – = not applicable, Q1 = first quarter, Q2 = second quarter, q-o-q = quarter-on-quarter, USD = United States dollar, y-o-y = year-on-year.

Notes:
1. Data reflect gross bond issuance.
2. Bloomberg LP end-of-period local currency–USD rates are used.
3   Growth rates are calculated from a local currency base and do not include currency effects. For emerging East Asia, growth figures are based on 30 June 2024 currency exchange rates and do not include currency effects.

Source: People's Republic of China (CEIC Data Company); Hong Kong, China (Hong Kong Monetary Authority); Indonesia (Bank Indonesia, Directorate General of Budget Financing and Risk Management, Ministry of Finance; and Indonesia Stock Exchange); Japan (Japan Securities Dealers Association); Republic of Korea (Bank of Korea and KG Zeroin Corporation); Malaysia (Bank Negara Malaysia); Philippines (Bureau of the Treasury and Bloomberg LP); Singapore (Monetary Authority of Singapore and Bloomberg LP); Thailand (Bank of Thailand and Thai Bond Market Association); and Viet Nam (Vietnam Bond Market Association and Bloomberg LP).

Section 3. Intra-Regional Bond Issuance

Intra-regional bond issuance in emerging East Asia rebounded on higher issuance from Hong Kong, China and the Republic of Korea.[4] The region's total intra-regional debt sales reached USD11.2 billion in Q2 2024 on growth of 27.1% q-o-q (**Figure 10**). Increased intra-regional bond issuance during the quarter was propelled by significant increases in Hong Kong, China and the Republic of Korea's intra-regional debt sales, offsetting decreased issuance from Singapore. The PRC and Malaysia both resumed their intra-regional bond issuance in Q2 2024, with total debt sales amounting to USD0.05 billion each. During the quarter, Hong Kong, China remained the top issuer of intra-regional bonds in emerging East Asia, accounting for 90.5% of the regional total. Hong Kong, China's total issuance increased 26.3% q-o-q to USD10.2 billion in Q2 2024 from USD8.0 billion in Q1 2024. Meanwhile, Singapore and the Republic of Korea's issuances accounted for 4.5% and 4.1%, respectively, of emerging East Asia's intra-regional total during the quarter. Singapore's total issuance declined 1.7% q-o-q to

USD0.5 billion, while the Republic of Korea's total issuance increased 68.5% q-o-q to USD0.5 billion in Q2 2024 from USD0.3 billion in Q1 2024. Among corporate issuers of intra-regional bonds during the quarter, China Merchants Group—a state-owned logistics firm based in Hong Kong, China—remained the top issuer in the region, with aggregate issuance of USD3.6 billion, which was equivalent to 31.8% of the regional total.

The transportation sector and CNY-denominated bonds continued to dominate the region's intra-regional bond issuance in Q2 2024. CNY-denominated issuance accounted for 98.3% (USD11.0 billion) of emerging East Asia's intra-regional quarterly total, while issuances denominated in Hong Kong dollars and Singapore dollars collectively accounted for only 1.7% (**Figure 11**). By sector, the transportation industry remained the largest issuer (USD4.3 billion) of intra-regional bonds during the quarter, comprising 38.4% of the region's total. This was followed by the financial sector (USD4.2 billion) with a 37.5% share of the market. The utilities sector was the third-largest issuer of intra-regional bonds in Q2 2024, with total issuance amounting to USD1.4 billion, or the equivalent of 12.6% of the region's intra-regional total.

Figure 10: Intra-Regional Bond Issuance in Select Emerging East Asian Economies

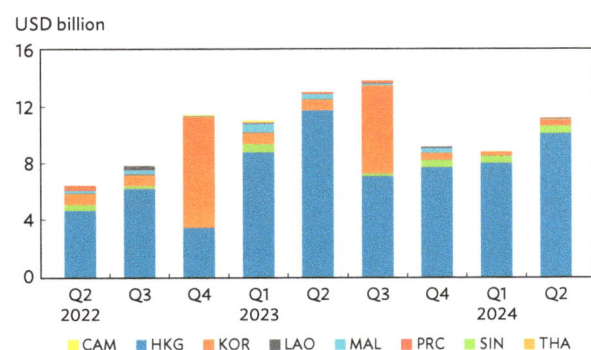

CAM = Cambodia; HKG = Hong Kong, China; KOR = Republic of Korea; LAO = Lao People's Democratic Republic; MAL = Malaysia; PRC = People's Republic of China; Q1 = first quarter; Q2 = second quarter; Q3 = third quarter; Q4 = fourth quarter; SIN = Singapore; THA = Thailand; USD = United States dollar.

Notes:
1. Emerging East Asia is defined to include member states of the Association of Southeast Asian Nations plus the People's Republic of China; Hong Kong, China; and the Republic of Korea.
2. Intra-regional bond issuance is defined as emerging East Asian bond issuance denominated in a regional currency excluding the issuer's home currency.
3. Figures were computed based on 30 June 2024 currency exchange rates and do not include currency effects.

Source: *AsianBondsOnline* calculations based on Bloomberg LP data.

Figure 11: Intra-Regional Bond Issuance in Emerging East Asia by Economy, Currency, and Sector in the Second Quarter of 2024

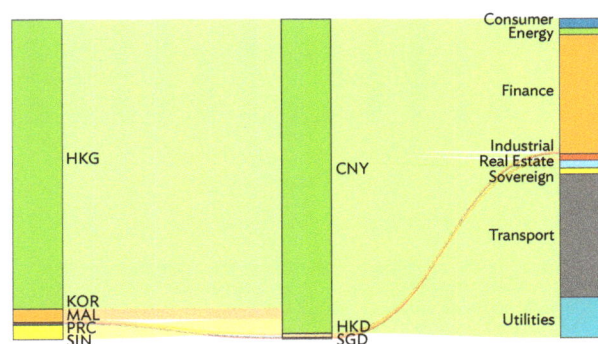

CNY = Chinese yuan; HKD = Hong Kong dollar; HKG = Hong Kong, China; KOR = Republic of Korea; MAL = Malaysia; PRC = People's Republic of China; SGD = Singapore dollar; SIN = Singapore.

Note: Intra-regional bond issuance is defined as emerging East Asian bond issuance denominated in a regional currency excluding the issuer's home currency.

Source: *AsianBondsOnline* calculations based on Bloomberg LP data.

---

[4] Intra-regional bond issuance is defined as emerging East Asian bond issuance denominated in a regional currency, excluding the issuer's home currency.

Section 4. G3 Currency Bond Issuance

In Q2 2024, issuance of G3 currency bonds in emerging East Asia soared to USD58.2 billion, reflecting a 47.7% increase from the previous quarter and a 45.5% increase from a year earlier (Figure 12).[5] The Republic of Korea was an exception, with its G3 currency bond issuance shrinking 35.8% q-o-q to USD8.8 billion. After recording weak issuance in Q1 2024, the PRC's G3 currency bond issuance surged 114.3% q-o-q to USD28.5 billion in Q2 2024, comprising 49.0% of all G3 currency bond issuance in emerging East Asia and making it the region's top G3 issuer during the quarter (**Figure 13**). The increased issuance by the PRC partially stemmed from more borrowing among the local financing vehicles of local governments amid increased demand from foreign bond investors. The PRC's Alibaba Group was the top G3 currency bond issuer, borrowing USD5.0 billion through a private offering for share buybacks. ASEAN markets totaled USD13.3 billion of G3 currency bond issuance, reflecting a 77.7% q-o-q increase and comprising 22.9% of the regional total. Indonesia retained the top spot within ASEAN with USD5.0 billion

worth of G3 issuance in Q2 2024, while Singapore replaced Malaysia in the second spot after issuing USD3.3 billion worth of G3 currency bonds.

Section 5. Yield Curve Movements

Between 1 June and 30 August, most government bond yield curves in emerging East Asia saw bullish flattening on moderating regional inflation, while economic growth remained largely stable (Figure 14). Moderating inflation during the review period, as well as expectations of a Federal Reserve rate cut in September, led to a bullish flattening in the yield curves of the Republic of Korea, the Philippines, Thailand, and Viet Nam. The PRC and Hong Kong, China also experienced the flattening of their yield curves, albeit due to slower economic gains in the PRC and a series of policy rate cuts by the People's Bank of China. The region's remaining markets saw a bear flattening of their respective yield curves. In addition to the PRC, the Philippines' central bank also reduced its policy rate during the review period, while central banks in all other markets awaited the Federal Reserve's expected rate cut before making any changes to their respective monetary policies.

Figure 13: G3 Currency Bond Issuance in Emerging East Asia in the Second Quarter of 2024

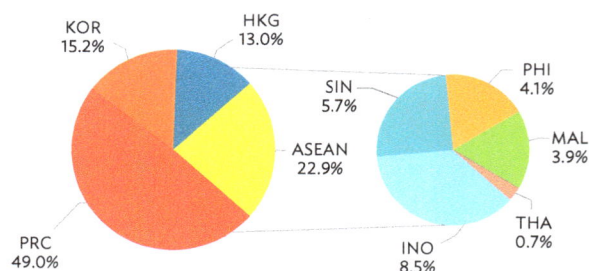

ASEAN = Association of Southeast Asian Nations; HKG = Hong Kong, China; INO = Indonesia; KOR = Republic of Korea; MAL = Malaysia; PHI = Philippines; PRC = People's Republic of China; SIN = Singapore; THA = Thailand.
Notes:
1. Emerging East Asia is defined to include member states of ASEAN plus the People's Republic of China; Hong Kong, China; and the Republic of Korea.
2. G3 currency bonds are denominated in either euros, Japanese yen, or United States dollars.
Source: *AsianBondsOnline* calculations based on Bloomberg LP data.

Figure 12: Monthly G3 Currency Bond Issuance in Select Emerging East Asian Markets

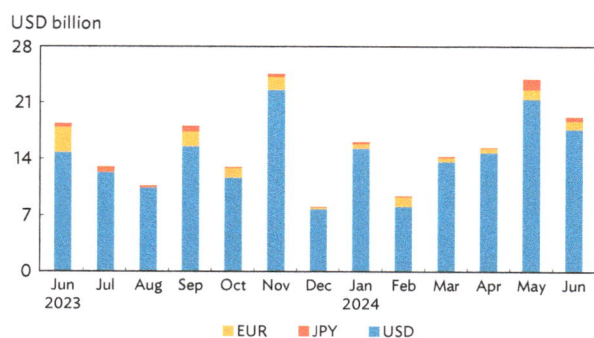

EUR = euro, JPY = Japanese yen, USD = United States dollar.
Notes:
1. Emerging East Asia is defined to include member states of the Association of Southeast Asian Nations plus the People's Republic of China; Hong Kong, China; and the Republic of Korea.
2. G3 currency bonds are denominated in either euros, Japanese yen, or United States dollars.
3. Figures were computed based on 30 June 2024 currency exchange rates and do not include currency effects.
Source: *AsianBondsOnline* calculations based on Bloomberg LP data.

---

[5] G3 currency bonds are bonds denominated in either euros, Japanese yen, or United States dollars.

Figure 14: Benchmark Yield Curves—Local Currency Government Bonds

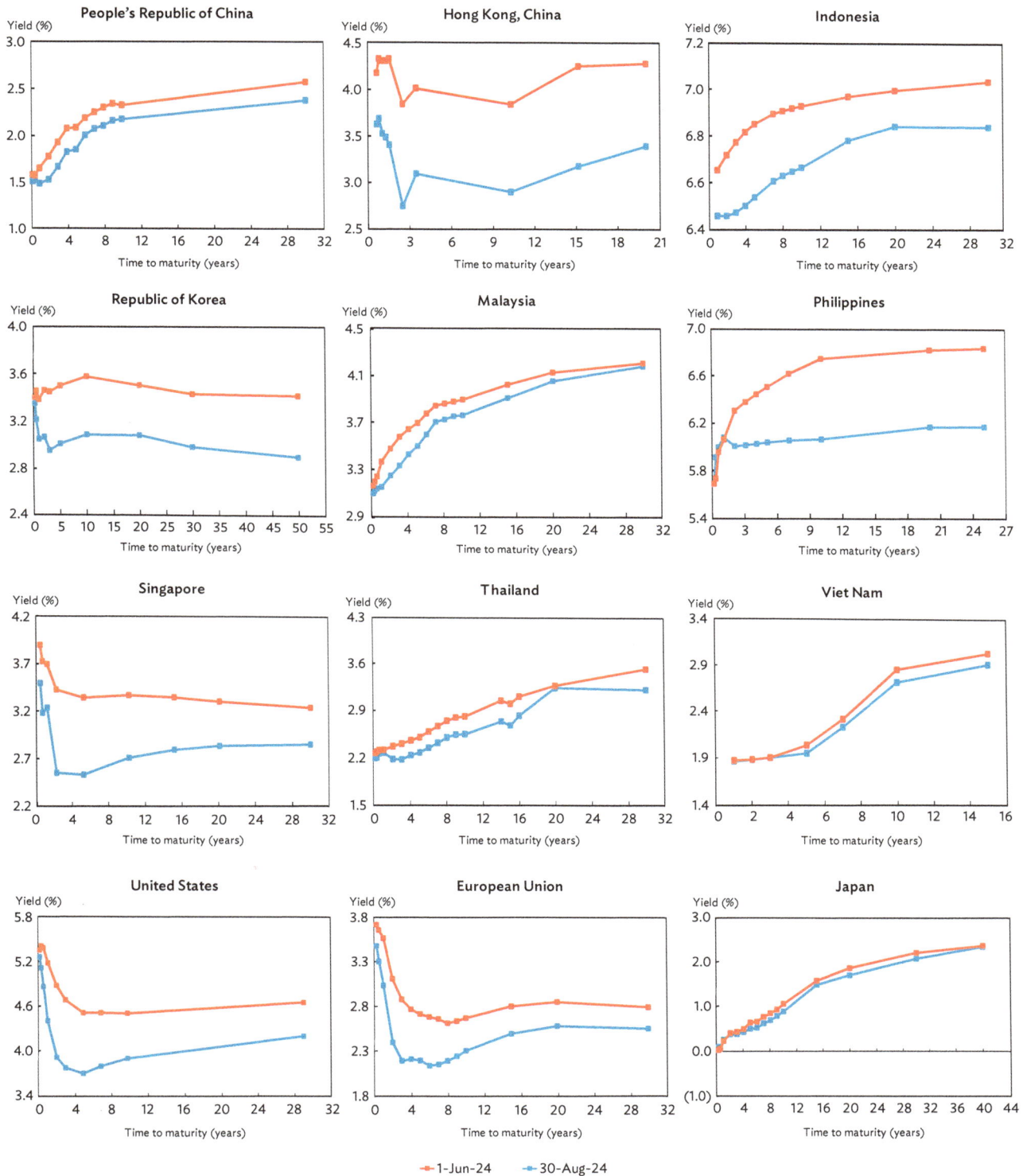

People's Republic of China

Hong Kong, China

Indonesia

Republic of Korea

Malaysia

Philippines

Singapore

Thailand

Viet Nam

United States

European Union

Japan

1-Jun-24   30-Aug-24

( ) = negative.
Sources: Based on data from Bloomberg LP and Thai Bond Market Association.

Recent Developments in ASEAN+3 Sustainable Bond Markets

Sustainable Bonds Outstanding

ASEAN+3's sustainable bonds outstanding reached USD868.1 billion at the end of June on a robust annual expansion of 17.4%.[6] ASEAN+3 market's expansion exceeded that of the European Union 20 (EU-20) (16.5%) and the global (17.0%) sustainable bond markets during the second quarter (Q2) of 2024. On a quarter-on-quarter (q-o-q) basis, however, the ASEAN+3 sustainable bond market's expansion moderated to 1.9% in Q2 2024 from 2.9% in the previous quarter due to a high volume of bond maturities. Association of Southeast Asian Nations (ASEAN) markets led the region in terms of quarterly growth at 6.4% q-o-q, supported by strong issuance. Meanwhile, ASEAN+3 accounted for 19.0% of total global sustainable bonds

outstanding at the end of June and remained the second-largest regional market after the EU-20 (36.9%) (**Figure 15**). Nevertheless, the ASEAN+3 sustainable bond market's relative size as a share of its general bond market is only 2.3%, which is much lower than the EU-20's corresponding share of 7.8%.

The ASEAN+3 sustainable bond market was dominated by green bonds, local currency (LCY) financing, and private sector participation at the end of June (Figure 16). In contrast to the EU-20, the ASEAN+3 sustainable bond market's issuer and currency profiles differ from those of the region's general bond market.

- By instrument, green bonds accounted for 61.6% of total sustainable bonds outstanding in ASEAN+3, followed by social bonds (18.2%), sustainability bonds (13.9%), and transition-related bonds (6.3%).

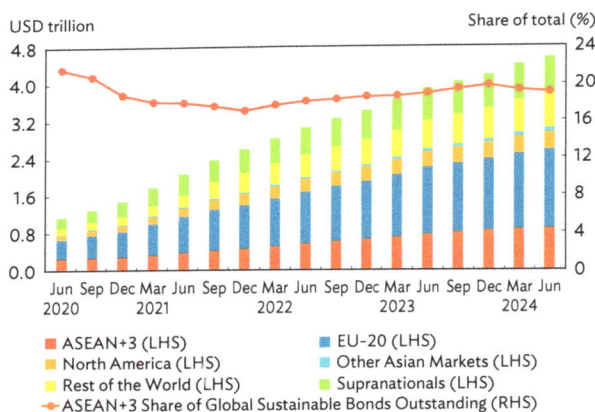

Figure 15: Global Sustainable Bonds Outstanding

ASEAN+3 = Association of Southeast Asian Nations plus the People's Republic of China; Hong Kong, China; Japan; and the Republic of Korea; EU-20 = European Union 20; LHS = left-hand side; RHS = right-hand side; USD = United States dollar.
Notes:
1. EU-20 includes European Union member markets Austria, Belgium, Croatia, Cyprus, Estonia, Finland, France, Germany, Greece, Ireland, Italy, Latvia, Lithuania, Luxembourg, Malta, the Netherlands, Portugal, Slovakia, Slovenia, and Spain.
2. Data include both local currency and foreign currency issues.
Source: *AsianBondsOnline* calculations based on Bloomberg LP data.

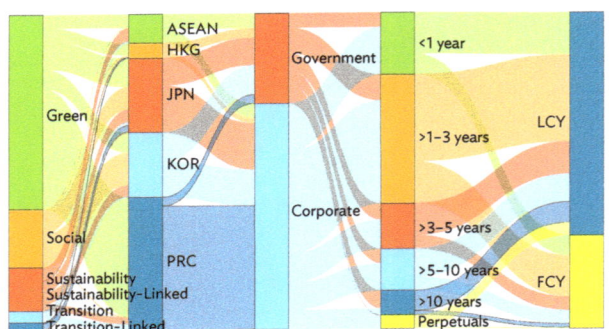

Figure 16: Market Profile of Outstanding ASEAN+3 Sustainable Bonds at the End of June 2024

ASEAN = Association of Southeast Asian Nations; FCY = foreign currency; HKG = Hong Kong, China; JPN = Japan; KOR = Republic of Korea; LCY = local currency; PRC = People's Republic of China.
Notes:
1. ASEAN+3 is defined to include member states of ASEAN plus the People's Republic of China; Hong Kong, China; Japan; and the Republic of Korea.
2. ASEAN comprises the markets of Cambodia, Indonesia, the Lao People's Democratic Republic, Malaysia, the Philippines, Singapore, Thailand, and Viet Nam.
Source: *AsianBondsOnline* calculations based on Bloomberg LP data.

---

[6] ASEAN+3 is defined to include member states of the Association of Southeast Asian Nations (ASEAN) plus the People's Republic of China; Hong Kong, China; Japan; and the Republic of Korea.

- By market, the People's Republic of China (PRC) accounted for 42.1% of ASEAN+3 sustainable bonds outstanding at the end of June, which was lower than PRC's share of 55.2% in the ASEAN+3 general bond market. ASEAN markets accounted for 9.2% of sustainable bonds outstanding in ASEAN+3, higher than their share of 6.0% in the ASEAN+3 general bond market.
- By issuer type, the private sector accounted for 71.5% of sustainable bonds outstanding at the end of Q2 2024, a stark contrast with its share of only 25.6% in the general bond market. In the EU-20, the private sector's presence does not differ as much between the sustainable and general bond markets as it does in ASEAN+3: At the end of Q2 2024, the private sector comprised 50.8% and 38.8% of the EU-20's sustainable bond market and general bond market, respectively. Within ASEAN+3, the public sector's presence in the sustainable bond market was highest in Hong Kong, China (62.3%) and ASEAN (51.7%).
- By currency, LCY-denominated bonds accounted for 70.2% of the ASEAN+3 sustainable bond market, well below the corresponding share of 96.7% in the general bond market. The LCY-denominated shares in the sustainable versus general bond markets are

much closer in the EU-20 than in ASEAN+3. In the EU-20, the LCY-denominated share in the sustainable bond market is 90.0%, similar to the 90.6% share in its general bond market.

The ASEAN+3 sustainable bond market largely comprises short- to medium-term financing. At the end of Q2 2024, about 74.6% of ASEAN+3 sustainable bonds outstanding carried tenors of 5 years or less, which was much more than the EU-20's share of 44.6% (**Figure 17**). These shorter-term tenors are most prevalent among social (80.0%), green (78.5%), and sustainability-linked (72.2%) bonds. Sustainable bonds outstanding in ASEAN markets have relatively longer tenors, with bonds bearing maturities of over 5 years accounting for 65.5% of total sustainable bonds outstanding at the end of June (**Figure 18**). The larger share of longer-term financing in ASEAN sustainable bond markets is mainly driven by the active participation of the public sector, which accounts for 51.7% of total bonds outstanding. Specifically, the governments of Indonesia, Singapore, and Thailand remain active issuers of sustainable bonds. Overall, ASEAN+3's sustainable bond market had a size-weighted average tenor of 4.3 years at the end of Q2 2024 (versus 8.1 years in the EU-20 and 7.6 years in the ASEAN+3

Figure 17: Maturity Profiles of ASEAN+3 and European Union 20 Sustainable Bonds Outstanding by Type of Bond at the End of June 2024

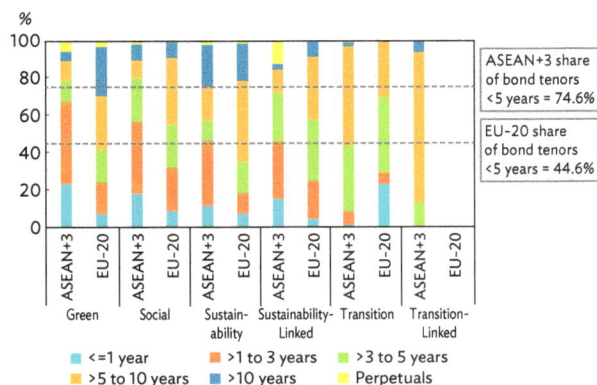

ASEAN+3 = Association of Southeast Asian Nations plus the People's Republic of China; Hong Kong, China; Japan; and the Republic of Korea; EU-20 = European Union 20.

Notes:
1. EU-20 includes European Union member markets Austria, Belgium, Croatia, Cyprus, Estonia, Finland, France, Germany, Greece, Ireland, Italy, Latvia, Lithuania, Luxembourg, Malta, the Netherlands, Portugal, Slovakia, Slovenia, and Spain.
2. Data include both local currency and foreign currency issues.

Source: *AsianBondsOnline* calculations based on Bloomberg LP data.

Figure 18: Maturity Profiles of ASEAN+3 and European Union 20 Sustainable Bonds Outstanding at the End of June 2024

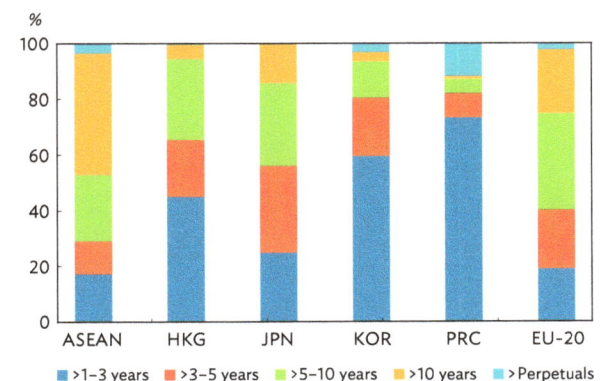

ASEAN+3 = Association of Southeast Asian Nations plus the People's Republic of China; Hong Kong, China; Japan; and the Republic of Korea; EU-20 = European Union 20; HKG = Hong Kong, China; JPN = Japan; KOR = Republic of Korea; PRC = People's Republic of China.

Notes:
1. The EU-20 includes European Union member markets Austria, Belgium, Croatia, Cyprus, Estonia, Finland, France, Germany, Greece, Ireland, Italy, Latvia, Lithuania, Luxembourg, Malta, the Netherlands, Portugal, Slovakia, Slovenia, and Spain.
2. Data include both local currency and foreign currency issues.

Source: *AsianBondsOnline* computations based on Bloomberg LP data.

general bond market). Meanwhile, the size-weighted average tenor in ASEAN was almost three times higher at 11.1 years. Within ASEAN, Singapore (16.7 years) and the Philippines (12.7 years) had the longest size-weighted average tenor.

Sustainable Bond Issuance

ASEAN+3 sustainable bond issuance rebounded to USD51.0 billion in Q2 2024, rising 1.6% q-o-q after contracting 10.7% q-o-q in the prior quarter. ASEAN+3's sustainable bond issuance accounted for 23.1% of the global total, up from 17.3% in the first quarter of 2024 (**Figure 19**). All sustainable bond types in ASEAN+3 posted q-o-q gains except for transition bonds. The most recent innovative bond instrument, transition-linked bonds, were issued by Japanese corporates to finance a total of USD0.4 billion in Q2 2024.[7] The PRC was the largest green and sustainability bond issuer in ASEAN+3 during the quarter, accounting for 69.2% and 39.9% of ASEAN+3's green and sustainability bond issuance, respectively. ASEAN markets were the second-largest issuer of both green bonds and sustainability bonds, with corresponding shares of 13.6% and 23.1%, respectively. Japan and the PRC dominated ASEAN+3

sustainability-linked bond issuance during the quarter, with comparable shares of 47.6% and 44.4%, respectively. Almost all transition bond (97.8%) and all transition-linked bond (100.0%) issuance during Q2 2024 came from Japan.

LCY-denominated, private sector, and shorter-term financing formed the bulk of sustainable bond issuance in ASEAN+3 during Q2 2024 (Figure 20).

- By currency, LCY bond issuance comprised 79.3% of the ASEAN+3 issuance total in Q2 2024, which was less than the LCY share of 94.7% in the general bond market during the same quarter. Again, the currency profile for sustainable bond issuance in the EU-20 was similar to that of the general bond market in Q2 2024. In the EU-20, the shares of LCY bond issuance in the sustainable (87.2%) and general (85.3%) bond markets were comparable.
- By maturity, 69.6% of ASEAN+3 sustainable bond issuance in Q2 2024 carried tenors of 5 years or less. These shorter-tenor issuances (5 years or less) were more prevalent in non-ASEAN economies (74.4%), while longer-tenor issuances (over 5 years) were more prevalent in ASEAN markets (70.6%).[8]

Figure 19: ASEAN+3 Sustainable Bond Issuance and Share of Global Total

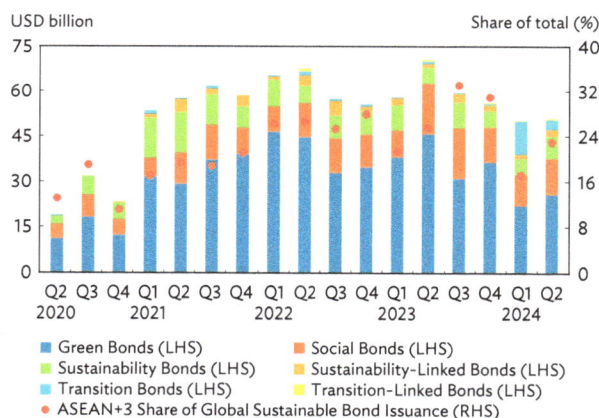

ASEAN+3 = Association of Southeast Asian Nations plus the People's Republic of China; Hong Kong, China; Japan; and the Republic of Korea; LHS = left-hand side; Q1 = first quarter; Q2 = second quarter; Q3 = third quarter; Q4 = fourth quarter; RHS = right-hand side; USD = United States dollar.
Note: Data include both local currency and foreign currency issues.
Source: *AsianBondsOnline* calculations based on Bloomberg LP data.

Figure 20: Market Profile of ASEAN+3 Sustainable Bond Issuance in the Second Quarter of 2024

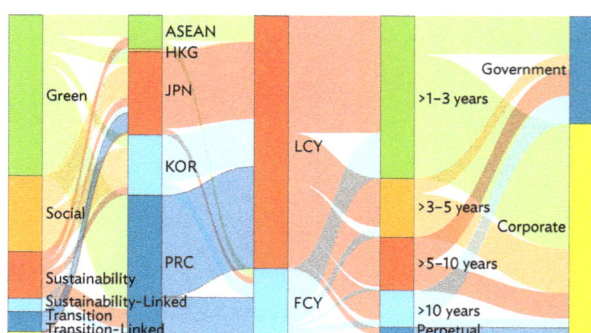

ASEAN = Association of Southeast Asian Nations; FCY = foreign currency; HKG = Hong Kong, China; JPN = Japan; KOR = Republic of Korea; LCY = local currency; PRC = People's Republic of China.
Notes:
1. ASEAN+3 is defined to include member states of ASEAN plus the People's Republic of China; Hong Kong, China; Japan; and the Republic of Korea.
2. ASEAN comprises the markets of Indonesia, Malaysia, the Philippines, Singapore, Thailand, and Viet Nam.
Source: *AsianBondsOnline* calculations based on Bloomberg LP data.

---

[7] Transition-linked bonds are sustainability-linked bonds in which one or more of the key performance indicators include monitoring greenhouse gas emission reductions.
[8] In the EU-20, bonds with maturities over 5 years comprised 79.0% of total sustainable bond issuance during the quarter, and those with shorter-term tenors had a 21.0% share.

The higher share of longer-term issuance in ASEAN markets is driven by the public sector, as nearly 80% of public sector issuance in ASEAN during Q2 2024 carried maturities of more than 5 years. ASEAN+3 sustainable bond issuance during the quarter had a size-weighted average tenor of 6.9 years, which was less than in the EU-20 sustainable bond market (9.6 years) and the ASEAN+3 general bond market (8.7 years). Meanwhile, the size-weighted average tenor of sustainable bond issuance in ASEAN markets in Q2 2024 was 18.0 years, due to active public sector issuance.

- Private sector issuance comprised 66.0% of total ASEAN+3 sustainable bond issuance in Q2 2024. While the public sector's issuance share during the quarter was relatively smaller, it comprised more longer-term bonds, accounting for 62.1% of sustainable bonds with tenors of more than 10 years. The private sector in ASEAN+3 was most active in green bond financing, accounting for 79.4% of ASEAN+3's green bond issuance (**Figure 21**). The public sector was a major issuer of ASEAN+3's social bond (59.8%) and transition bond (70.4%) issuance in Q2 2024. Financial institutions were the dominant private sector issuer during the quarter, accounting for 38.9% of total private sector sustainable bond issuance.

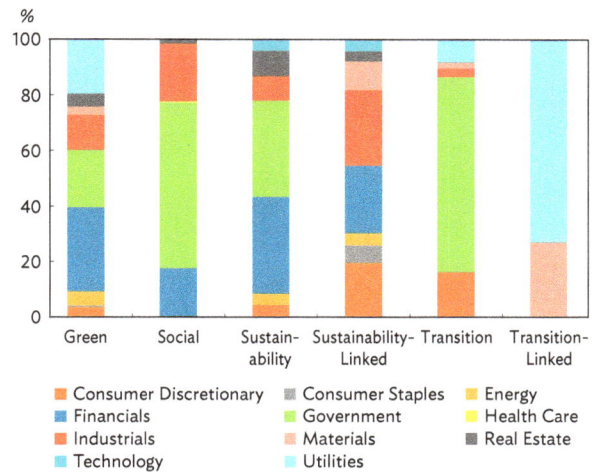

Figure 21: ASEAN+3 Sustainable Bond Issuance by Sector in the Second Quarter of 2024

Legend:
- Consumer Discretionary
- Consumer Staples
- Energy
- Financials
- Government
- Health Care
- Industrials
- Materials
- Real Estate
- Technology
- Utilities

Notes:
1. ASEAN+3 is defined to include member states of the Association of Southeast Asian Nations plus the People's Republic of China; Hong Kong, China; Japan; and the Republic of Korea.
2. Data include both local currency and foreign currency issues.
Source: *AsianBondsOnline* computations based on Bloomberg LP data.

Policy and Regulatory Developments

People's Republic of China

The People's Republic of China Eases Rules on Foreign Bond Issuance

On 23 July, the National Development and Reform Commission issued new rules easing the issuance of overseas corporate bonds. Under the new rules, qualified companies will be allowed to issue bonds under more relaxed financial standards and streamlined review processes. However, to be qualified issuers, companies must be ranked within the top five of their industry in terms of revenue and maintain a good credit rating, among other requirements.

Hong Kong, China

The Hong Kong Monetary Authority and the People's Bank of China Sign Memorandum of Understanding on Cross-Boundary Linkage of Payment Systems

On 2 August, the People's Bank of China and the Hong Kong Monetary Authority signed a memorandum of understanding to establish a cooperative framework for a cross-boundary linkage of payment systems between the People's Republic of China (PRC) and Hong Kong, China. The cross-boundary payment link is part of a series of measures announced in January to promote financial connectivity between the two markets.

Indonesia

Bank Indonesia Increases Frequency of Central Bank Bills Auction

In May, Bank Indonesia announced that it would increase the frequency of the auction of its Bank Indonesia Rupiah Securities from once a week to twice a week. The move is meant to attract additional capital flows and help maintain the stability of the rupiah.

Republic of Korea

The Republic of Korea Announces Economic Policy Directions for the Second Half of 2024

On 3 July, the Government of the Republic of Korea announced its economic policy directions for the second half of 2024. Economic growth for the year is expected to be 2.6%, up from the January forecast of 2.2%, supported by strong exports and a slowdown in inflation. To achieve this goal, the government announced that it will allot KRW25.0 trillion for various programs to help small business owners, including the reduction of financial costs and ways to improve their competitiveness. It will also allocate KRW5.6 trillion to ease the pressure of high living costs, in line with its policy of achieving price stability and strengthening domestic consumption. Lastly, it will increase public sector investments and loans by KRW15.0 trillion to support the domestic economy.

Malaysia

Malaysia Announces Fiscal Consolidation Plans

On 23 July, the Government of Malaysia announced its commitment to reduce its debt over the next 5 years, targeting a debt-to-gross-domestic-product ratio of 60.0%, down from the current ratio of 64.0%. In line with this, the government stated that it had begun reducing its annual net borrowings from about MYR100.0 billion in both 2021 and 2022 to MYR93.0 billion in 2023, and plans to further lower the target to MYR86.0 billion in 2024. Consequently, the ratio of the annual fiscal deficit to gross domestic product also decreased from 5.6% in 2022 to 5.0% in 2023, and is projected to decline to 4.3% in 2024.

Philippines

The Philippines Aims for Emerging Markets Bond Index Inclusion

In August, the Government of the Philippines discussed with JP Morgan Chase & Co. the inclusion of the government's locally issued PHP-denominated securities in JP Morgan's Emerging Markets Bond Index. The government expects that inclusion would encourage more participation from foreign investors and potentially bring an additional USD10.0 billion–USD12.0 billion in new portfolio flows into the government bond market.

The Philippine Government Seeks to Tap Foreign Debt Market

In July, the Government of the Philippines announced plans to tap the international debt market to raise the remaining USD3.0 billion needed for its 2024 borrowing program. The bonds will be denominated in United States dollars, euros, and Japanese yen, and will be issued in tranches, with the samurai bonds expected to be borrowed last. Of the USD3.0 billion target, about USD500.0 million will be raised through the offering of samurai bonds. The Philippines last issued samurai bonds in April 2022, with total debt sales amounting to JPY70.1 billion.

Singapore

Monetary Authority of Singapore and People's Bank of China Collaborate on Green and Transition Finance Initiatives

On 20 May, the Monetary Authority of Singapore and the People's Bank of China held the 2nd China–Singapore Green Finance Taskforce (GFTF) meeting in Beijing. The GFTF focuses on initiatives to scale up green and transition financing flows between Singapore and the PRC, and across the region. One of the initiatives discussed in the meeting was collaborating on a "green corridor" to encourage green panda bond issuances to meet the demand from Singapore issuers in the PRC's onshore bond market. The Monetary Authority of Singapore supports such financing flows through grant schemes like the Sustainable Bond Grant Scheme. The GFTF is seen as a key platform for the PRC and Singapore to jointly develop concrete initiatives to advance cooperation in green finance.

Thailand

Bank of Japan and Bank of Thailand Renew Bilateral Swap Arrangement

On 23 July, the Bank of Japan and the Bank of Thailand announced the renewal of the existing bilateral swap arrangement between Japan and Thailand. The arrangement allows the two monetary authorities to swap their respective local currencies in exchange for United States dollars. It also enables Thailand to swap Thai baht for Japanese yen. The size of the arrangement remained unchanged at up to USD3 billion or its equivalent in Japanese yen.

Viet Nam

State Bank of Vietnam Extends Policy on Debt Repayment Rescheduling

In June, the State Bank of Vietnam extended the enforcement of Circular No. 2 until 31 December 2024 from an original end date of 30 June 2024. Circular No. 2 allows financial institutions to reschedule debt repayment periods and maintain debt categories for certain sectors to support struggling businesses amid rising levels of bad debt.

Climate Finance Policy Support for Mobilizing Transition Finance in Asia

Transition finance has emerged as one of the fastest growing and most hotly debated areas in sustainable finance. This reflects a growing awareness and acceptance in the market that certain high-emitting sectors like steel, cement, shipping, and aviation are by their nature "hard to abate" due to current technological limitations and cost or feasibility considerations; yet, these sectors are also non-substitutable and too economically critical to phase out. At the same time, the pressure on investors to "go green," resulting from stricter climate sustainability requirements and accelerated carbon phase-out policies, necessarily raises the apparent risk of continued investment in these assets, thus reducing investment appetites and crowding out necessary transition investments.

Managing this challenge is particularly pressing for developing economies in Asia and the Pacific, which are often reliant on these heavy industries but lack access to sufficient financial and technological resources for navigating their transition. Accordingly, Asian policy makers and market regulators have emerged as global leaders in promoting transition finance opportunities for their economies, while also attempting to address the key challenges issuers and investors face.

Key challenges and risk that regulators need to address when developing transition finance policies include the following:

(1) a current lack of generally agreed definitions across jurisdictions for transition finance and corporate transition plans, which can conflict with traditional approaches to green finance while limiting market standardization and the potential for cross-border financing and investment flows;

(2) reputational risks to investors, who may face greenwashing accusations for providing financing to high-emitting sectors and activities, as upfront financed emissions often increase as a result; unlike green or zero-emission investments, there is no single accepted metric for differentiating legitimate transition assets from business-as-usual assets;

(3) stranded-asset risks to corporates, which bear the risk of potential losses from investments in alternative and ultimately non-commercially viable transition technologies, or misallocated capital expenditures designed to prolong the life of unsustainable operations and technologies, especially in an accelerated net zero transition scenario; and

(4) the need for detailed technical standards, either in the form of sectoral technology roadmaps or transition taxonomies with technical and temporal screening thresholds that are often dependent on the economy- and development-level context, and transition plan frameworks for corporates to communicate to investors that their transition strategies are feasible and credible.

Regulatory Approaches Defining Transition Finance: Taxonomies and Roadmaps

A common thread in transition finance is how regulators can balance the need to channel capital into hard-to-abate sectors and breakthrough research and development to achieve a just and achievable carbon transition, while also maintaining a robust and science-based green finance framework that is credible to sustainable investors and discourages greenwashing. Currently, two main approaches have emerged: transition taxonomies and transition sector technology roadmaps (**Table 3**).[9]

In some cases, regulatory bodies are developing general mandates or voluntary guidelines for corporates to produce transition plans for investors to assess actual

---

This special section was prepared by Jason Mortimer, head of sustainable investment and fixed income and senior portfolio manager at Nomura Asset Management.

[9] CFA Institute Research and Policy Center. 2024. *Navigating Transition Finance: An Action List.*

Table 3: Regulatory Approaches for Transition Finance

	Transition Taxonomy	Technology Roadmap
Description	Expansion of conventional green taxonomies to recognize intermediate categories for transitional or enabling activities and technologies, subject to technical standards, time constraints, or designated sectors	Economy- and sector-specific guidance on technological development and implementation roadmaps with target time frames for decarbonization in certain high-emitting sectors
Example Methodologies	"Traffic light systems" with an intermediate category for activities that are on a path to becoming sustainable for the climate or facilitating significant emissions reductions (i.e., green, amber, red [ineligible]) Technical screening criteria such as emissions intensity and time limits Principles-based designations of activities and sectors by tiers and classes of transition Catalogs or lists of transitional and/or enabling-activity technologies	Technological development pathways with timelines, target emission reduction levels, and necessary enabling technologies with multiple possible approaches
Implementation Examples in Force	• MAS–Asia Taxonomy • ASEAN Taxonomy V2 • BNM Malaysia Climate-Change and Principle-based Taxonomy • Thailand Green and Transition Taxonomy • Indonesia Green Taxonomy Edition 1 • Republic of Korea K-Taxonomy • People's Republic of China (local level)	• METI Japan Sector Technology Roadmaps for GHG-Intensive Industries
Implementation Pending or Under Discussion	Australia, Canada, People's Republic of China (national level)	

ASEAN = Association of Southeast Asian Nations; BNM = Bank Negara Malaysia; GHG = greenhouse gas emissions; MAS = Monetary Authority of Singapore; METI = Ministry of Economy, Trade and Industry.

Note: All descriptions as of March 2024.

Sources: Author's compilation based on data from CFA Institute Research and Policy Center. 2024. *Navigating Transition Finance: An Action List*; and Net Zero. 2023. *Regulation Stocktake Report*.

progress and planned steps for achieving net zero pledges.[10] This approach can complement and reinforce transition taxonomies and technology roadmaps, as well as align the jurisdiction's corporate disclosures with international climate-related disclosure standards such as the International Financial Reporting Standards Foundation S2 Climate-Related Disclosures (**Table 4**).[11]

Japan's Comprehensive Approach to Transition Finance Polices

While many economies and regions have focused on definitional methods by adopting green taxonomies to include transition elements or categories, Japan has taken an altogether different approach by directly providing technological guidance with an array of potential transition pathways specifically developed for its own economy. In fact, Japan's industrial and energy sector transition roadmaps from the Ministry of Economy, Trade and Industry are part of a larger package of pro-growth, carbon-pricing reforms and society-wide decarbonization strategies called the Green Transformation, or GX Policy, for meeting the market's long-term growth and energy security goals. This national green development policy is backed by a JPY150 trillion package of long-term public–private financing from the issuance of the world's first sovereign Climate Transition Bonds, or GX Japanese Government Bonds, as part of a 10-year funding strategy led by the Ministry of Finance.[12]

[10] Climate Governance Initiative. 2024. *Transition Planning: A Global Outlook for Board Directors.*

[11] Net Zero Climate. 2023. *Regulation Stocktake Report*. https://netzeroclimate.org/wp-content/uploads/2023/11/Net-Zero-Regulation-Stocktake-Report-November-2023.pdf.

[12] Government of Japan, Ministry of Economy, Trade and Industry. Transition Finance Overview (accessed 31 July 2024).

**Table 4: Jurisdictions with Regulatory Requirements
for Corporate Transition Plans**

In Place	• Brazil: Central bank mandates that financial institutions provide a TP • European Union: CSRD mandates that large corporates and investors disclose TPs • France: National financial regulator has produced a TP guide for business • Japan: Corporate governance code encourages disclosure of TPs and pathways • Russian Federation: State companies must disclose TP; central bank issued a TP methodology • Türkiye: Entities must disclose transition strategies on a comply-or-explain basis • UK: Transition Planning Task Force developing "gold standard" for TPs
In Progress	Australia, Canada, Germany, India, Indonesia, Italy, Republic of Korea, South Africa

CSRD = Corporate Sustainability Reporting Directive, TP = transition plan, UK = United Kingdom.
Note: All descriptions as of March 2024.
Sources: Author's compilation based on Net Zero. 2023. *Regulation Stocktake Report*; and Climate Governance Initiative. 2024. *Transition Planning: A Global Outlook for Board Directors*.

This ambitious and comprehensive package of financial and industrial policies arguably positions Japan as an advanced proponent of transition finance. However, the GX strategy has also attracted controversy for including natural gas and nuclear power as part of an "all of the above" energy decarbonization approach. The strategy also includes emerging technologies like carbon sequestration and ammonia co-firing for coal plant and fossil fuel phase-out strategies. This experience illustrates the need for policymakers to clearly and honestly communicate why climate transition strategies are necessary, with the risks and benefits that they entail.

Conclusion

Overall, there is growing consensus that sustainable finance policies need to channel capital for both green and transition investments to achieve an orderly and affordable climate transition. In some cases, it has become necessary to carefully rework and redefine certain climate finance regulations to de-risk and provide appropriate support to transition sectors and development pathways. For their part, corporates in hard-to-abate sectors and sustainable investors alike can benefit from better disclosure of credible transition plans and guidance of where to extend financing for climate- and commercially viable transition pathways. By delivering practical climate transition policies with a focus on addressing the key challenges to market participants, policy makers and regulators can effectively expand green finance to incorporate transition elements while upholding sustainable market integrity.

Hedging Climate-Related Risks: Role of Insurance

Introduction

The challenge of climate change is one of the most significant issues of our time, affecting not only environmental systems but also the global economy and financial markets. The occurrence of climate extremes represents an existential crisis for those who hold assets and the insurers who underwrite their risk. In recent years, there have been in excess of 1,000 extreme weather events globally that have caused more than USD1 trillion in damages.[13]

Figure 22 depicts the trend of insured losses by cause and year. In 2022, the global insurance industry was expected to experience a significant increase in natural-catastrophe-related claims, with such claims projected to reach 54% above the 10-year average and 115% above the 30-year average (Fantini et al. 2024). In this context, the insurance industry occupies a unique position, assuming a dual role in both the mitigation of risks and the exploration of opportunities presented by the climate crisis.

This note is based on a forthcoming paper by the author that explores these dimensions through an in-depth analysis of the ways in which the insurance sector can adapt to the evolving landscape of climate risks, while simultaneously contributing to the broader societal effort to combat climate change.

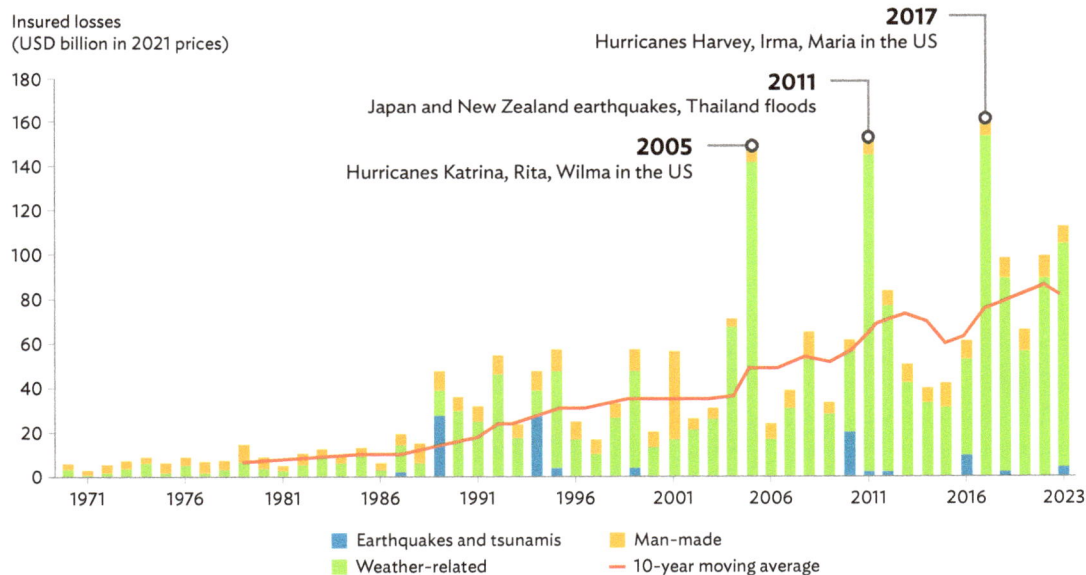

Figure 22: Insured Losses by Cause and Year

Insured losses (USD billion in 2021 prices)

2017 — Hurricanes Harvey, Irma, Maria in the US

2011 — Japan and New Zealand earthquakes, Thailand floods

2005 — Hurricanes Katrina, Rita, Wilma in the US

Legend: Earthquakes and tsunamis — Man-made — Weather-related — 10-year moving average

US = United States, USD = United States dollar.
Source: Adapted from Wagner, Katherine R.H. 2022. Designing Insurance for Climate Change. *Nature Climate Change* 12 (12): 1070–72.

This note was prepared by Suk Hyun (head professor) at the Graduate School of Environmental Finance of Yonsei University.

[13] *Bloomberg*. 2024. Natural Disasters Led to $250 Billion in Global Losses Last Year.

Literature Review: The Role of Insurance in Climate Change Management

The Multifaceted Role of Insurance

This literature review illuminates the multifaceted role that the insurance industry plays in the management of climate-related risks. Historically, insurance has been a vital means of providing financial protection against disasters triggered by natural hazards and other catastrophic events. However, the increasing frequency and severity of these events due to climate change necessitates a more proactive approach from insurers.

Notable studies, including those by Mills (2009) and Jarzabkowski et al. (2019), emphasize the necessity for insurance companies to implement adaptation strategies that foster resilience not only within their own operations but also across the broader economy. For example, Mills' study catalogued the various insurance products and services that have been developed in response to climate change, emphasizing the importance of green remediation and the necessity of addressing gaps in coverage. Similarly, Jarzabkowski et al. (2019) argued for the development of open-source climate risk models and the integration of these models into national strategies, emphasizing the role of insurance in both physical and financial adaptation to climate change.

Economic Impacts and Risk Management

The economic consequences of climate change are considerable and pervasive, impacting a multitude of sectors, including agriculture, infrastructure, and beyond. The study examines the potential for insurance to play a pivotal role in mitigating the impacts of climate change through effective risk management. For example, Michel-Kerjan's (2010) evaluation of the National Flood Insurance Program identifies areas where insurance programs can be improved to enhance their effectiveness in managing climate-related risks. Furthermore, Surminski (2014) underscores the significance of flood insurance in risk reduction, emphasizing the necessity for substantial enhancements to optimize its efficacy in mitigating the direct risks associated with flooding events.

The financial implications of climate change extend beyond the immediate recovery from disasters. As Campiglio et al. (2023) observe, the revaluation of financial assets due to climate-related risks has significant implications for financial stability. This highlights the necessity for continuous assessment and adjustment of financial assets and market premiums to account for evolving risks.

Climate Change Risks and Insurers' Risk Management

Managing Physical and Transitional Risks

Climate change risks can be reflected in various aspects of an insurance company's operations, including insurance risk, market risk, investment risk, and reputational risk. The increasing frequency and severity of disasters due to climate change can lead to a rise in insurance payouts, affecting the financial stability of insurers. To manage these risks, insurers must adopt strategies such as geographic diversification and reinsurance.

Reinsurance, in particular, plays a crucial role in maintaining resilience against climate-related risks. By distributing their exposure across diverse geographical regions, insurers can mitigate the financial impact of localized disasters. However, the forthcoming study notes that smaller insurers may face challenges due to increased reinsurance premiums, which could lead to market consolidation and the dominance of larger insurers.

The Impact on Life and Health Insurance

Climate change also has implications for life and health insurance, as extreme weather events can result in elevated mortality rates among high-risk individuals. Insurers must adjust their underwriting criteria to account for these heightened risks, particularly in the context of long-term climate change. Additionally, changes in crop and fish species due to climate change can impact loss rates and profitability for insurers in sectors such as agriculture and fisheries.

The role of reinsurance in managing these long-term risks is emphasized, as it provides diversification benefits that help insurers maintain resilience. However, the study cautions that the increasing frequency and intensity of extreme weather events may result in higher reinsurance premiums, which could pose challenges for smaller insurers.

Climate Change Risk and Asset Management

The Impact of Climate Risks on Investment Portfolios

Climate change affects insurers' asset management, particularly through changes in company valuations driven by the transition to a low-carbon economy. The implementation of low-carbon policies is expected to reduce the value of traditional industries, such as fossil fuels, while increasing the value of green industries. Insurers must adjust their investment portfolios to reflect these changes, reallocating assets to increase their holdings of green financial assets.

Even traditionally safe assets, such as government bonds, are not immune to climate risks. The study discusses how disasters triggered by natural hazards can lead to economic slowdowns, potentially resulting in downgrades of sovereign credit ratings. This is particularly relevant for bonds issued by economies that have experienced or are expected to experience severe disasters triggered by natural hazards. The study also highlights the risks associated with municipal bonds, which are contingent upon the degree of government and municipal response to disasters triggered by natural hazards.

Real Estate and Climate Risks

The study also addresses the impact of climate change on the real estate sector, noting that shifts in governmental policies and regulations related to energy efficiency can influence the value of real estate assets. The study suggests that insurers must remain agile in their asset management strategies, adjusting their portfolios to account for both physical and transitional risks associated with climate change.

The Expanding Role of Insurance in Climate Adaptation

Engaging in Risk Management Across Sectors

The role of the insurance industry in climate adaptation is evolving in response to the growing risks associated with climate change. The insurance industry is increasingly regarded as a pivotal actor in risk management across a spectrum of sectors within the real economy, encompassing manufacturing and services. This expanded role is driven by two key factors: (i) the increased occurrence of disasters triggered by natural hazards and (ii) the growing awareness of climate risks among businesses and governments.

International organizations have acknowledged the pivotal role of the financial sector, including insurance, in addressing climate change. For example, the Financial Stability Board constituted a task force in 2015 to investigate responses to climate change risks, and the European Union initiated an action plan on sustainable finance in 2018. These initiatives highlight the vital role of the insurance industry in mitigating climate risks through the development of innovative financial instruments and risk management strategies.

Systematic Integration of Climate Risk Management

To effectively address climate risks, insurance companies must systematically integrate climate risk management into their business models. This involves recognizing climate change as a fundamental risk factor in insurance underwriting, asset management, and corporate social responsibility efforts. The rise in disasters caused by climate change, often accompanied by significant financial losses, necessitates a comprehensive approach to risk management that considers both physical and transitional risks.

Physical risks include phenomena such as global warming, sea level rise, and disasters like storms, floods, and wildfires. These risks have the potential to disrupt national economic infrastructure, leading to reduced economic activity and the transfer of risk to financial markets. The study highlights the importance of understanding these risks at a macroeconomic level, as their ripple effects can have profound implications for the insurance industry.

Transitional risks, on the other hand, stem from policy shifts toward a low-carbon economy. These risks can significantly impact industries that are slow to adapt to new regulations and technological advancements. The study discusses how policy shifts, such as those mandated by the 2015 Paris Climate Agreement, can alter the economic behavior of market participants and increase market risk. Insurance companies must adapt to these changes by incorporating transitional risks into their risk assessment models and adjusting their investment portfolios accordingly.

Opportunities and Challenges for the Insurance Industry

Framework for Climate Risk Management

A framework for climate risk management has been developed with the objective of assisting insurers in the more effective management of the risks associated with climate change. The framework is structured around three principal stages: (i) before underwriting, (ii) before claims, and (iii) during or after claims.

Prior to the underwriting process, it is recommended that insurers develop more sophisticated modeling techniques and customer segmentation strategies to enhance their risk assessment capabilities. Furthermore, the study underscores the significance of product innovation, including the introduction of temporary coverage and parametric insurance, in addressing the evolving risks associated with climate change.

Prior to the occurrence of a claim, the study recommends the transfer of alternative risks through reinsurance, insurance pools, and insurance-linked securities. Furthermore, the study proposes the implementation of empirical studies and pilot programs to evaluate the efficacy of preventive measures and their impact on risk profiles.

In the period following a claim, insurers focus on reducing the cost of settling claims in the event of a catastrophe. This can be achieved through the provision of consulting services, the dissemination of risk awareness tools, and the implementation of real-time notifications and support mechanisms. Furthermore, the study highlights the importance of incorporating enhanced resilience measures into post-disaster reconstruction efforts.

Increasing Awareness and Response Among Insurance Companies

There is a discrepancy in climate risk awareness among companies, which is influenced by their exposure to different insurance categories and a general lack of awareness. Nevertheless, as the climate crisis intensifies,

there is a growing awareness of the issue. It is incumbent upon each insurance company to analyze climate risk in accordance with its business model and develop a strategy that is aligned with this analysis. The crisis underscores the necessity for insurance companies to prioritize the reduction of Scope 3 greenhouse gas emissions, which are predominantly associated with their investments. In anticipation of mandatory sustainable disclosures, insurers must ascertain and differentiate between Scope 1, 2, and 3 emissions as illustrated in **Figure 23**, with a particular emphasis on distinguishing between financed emissions from asset management and insurance-related emissions from underwriting. Addressing both types is vital for attaining carbon neutrality, although facilitated emissions are less pertinent for insurers.

Conclusion

The study provides a comprehensive overview of the insurance industry's role in managing climate change risks. By adopting proactive risk management strategies and capitalizing on new business opportunities, the insurance industry can play a key role in mitigating the impacts of climate change while enhancing its own resilience and profitability. The study's framework for climate risk management, combined with the industry's growing awareness of climate risks, highlights the need for a systematic and integrated approach to managing climate-related risks.

The public sector has a critical role to play in supporting the growth of the insurance sector during the transition to a low-carbon economy by providing subsidies, tax incentives, and a regulatory framework that reduces the financial burden on insurers, thereby enabling lower premiums for consumers. They can also establish public–private partnerships to share risks, invest in technology and data infrastructure to improve risk modeling, and promote green bonds and insurance-linked securities to diversify insurers' portfolios. In addition, educational campaigns are raising awareness of climate risks and the benefits of insurance, leading to broader market penetration and, ultimately, more affordable insurance premiums.

Figure 23: Conceptualization of Scope 1, 2, and 3 Emissions

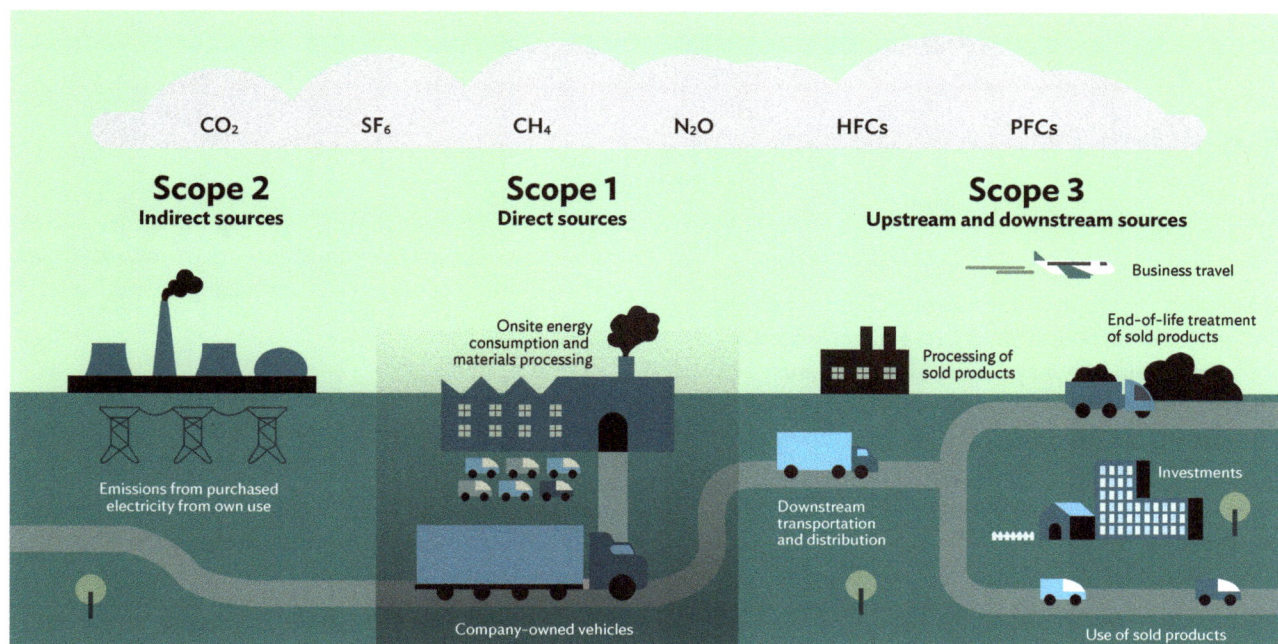

CH₄ = methane, CO₂ = carbon dioxide, HCFs = hydrofluorocarbons, N₂O = nitrous oxide, NF₃ = nitrogen trifluoride, PFCs = perfluorinated compounds, SF₆ = sulfur hexafluoride.
Source: Oliver Wyman Forum. The Climate Action Navigator.

References

Campiglio, Emanuele, Louis Daumas, Pierre Monnin, and Adrian von Jagow. 2022. Climate-Related Risks in Financial Assets. *Journal of Economic Surveys* 37 (3): 950–52.

Fantini, Lorenzo, Blaisiane Blanchard, Sebastian Rath, Philippe Removille, Simone Schwemer, and Frederik Mayeres. 2023. An Insurance Risk Framework for Climate Adaptation. BCG, December 4.

Jarzabkowski, Paula, Konstantinos Chalkias, Daniel Clarke, Ekhosuehi Iyahen, Daniel Stadtmueller, Astrid Zwick. Insurance for Climate Adaptation: Opportunities and Limitations. Global Commission on Adaptation Background Paper.

Michel-Kerjan, Erwann. 2010. Catastrophe Economics: The National Flood Insurance Program. *Journal of Economic Perspectives* 24 (4): 165–86.

Mills, Evan. 2009. A Global Review of Insurance Industry Responses to Climate Change. *The Geneva Papers on Risk and Insurance* 34 (2009): 323–59.

Surminski, Swenja. 2014. The Role of Insurance in Reducing Direct Risk: The Case of Flood Insurance. *International Review of Environmental and Resource Economics* 7 (3–4): 241–78.

Market Summaries

People's Republic of China

Yield Movements

The People's Republic of China's (PRC) local currency (LCY) government bond yield curve experienced a bullish flattening between 1 June and 30 August as economic growth slowed and the central bank reduced key interest rates amid low inflation. The PRC's yield decline averaged 18 basis points (bps) across all maturities (**Figure 1**). The decline was largely due to softening economic growth, with the PRC's second quarter (Q2) gross domestic product growth rate falling to 4.7% year-on-year (y-o-y) from 5.3% y-o-y in the previous quarter. This, coupled with subdued inflation of 0.5% y-o-y in July (up slightly from 0.2% y-o-y in June), led to the People's Bank of China (PBOC) unexpectedly cutting a series of interest rates in July. The PBOC reduced by 10 bps each the 7-day repurchase rate, the 1-year loan prime rate, and the 5-year loan prime rate on 22 July. On 25 July, the PBOC lowered the 1-year medium-term lending facility rate by 20 bps to 2.3%. The PBOC has also recently expressed concern that rising government bond prices

are generating an asset bubble. In response, the central bank has discussed the importance of an upward sloping yield curve and considered discouraging or limiting further bond trades.

Local Currency Bond Market Size and Issuance

Growth in the PRC's LCY bond market accelerated in Q2 2024 on robust issuance by the government. Total LCY bonds outstanding grew 2.2% quarter-on-quarter (q-o-q) in Q2 2024, up from 1.2% q-o-q in the first quarter (Q1), to a reach size of CNY145.1 trillion (**Figure 2**). While both types of bonds grew in Q2 2024, gains in government bonds quickened to 2.8% q-o-q from 1.2% q-o-q in Q1 2024 as the government began issuing special long-term Treasury bonds to support the economy. In contrast, corporate bond market growth slowed to 0.9% q-o-q in Q2 2024 from 1.2% q-o-q in the previous quarter.

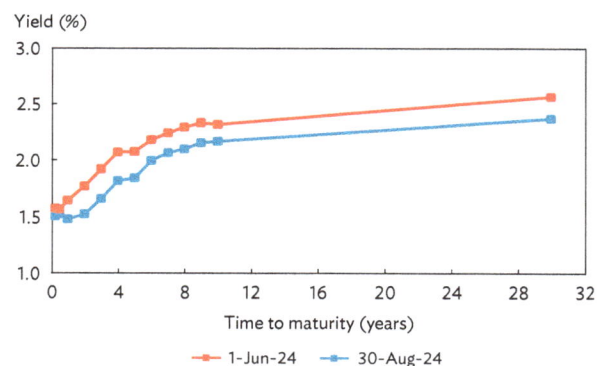

Figure 1: The People's Republic of China's Benchmark Yield Curve—Local Currency Government Bonds

Yield (%)

Time to maturity (years)

—■— 1-Jun-24   —■— 30-Aug-24

Source: Based on data from Bloomberg LP.

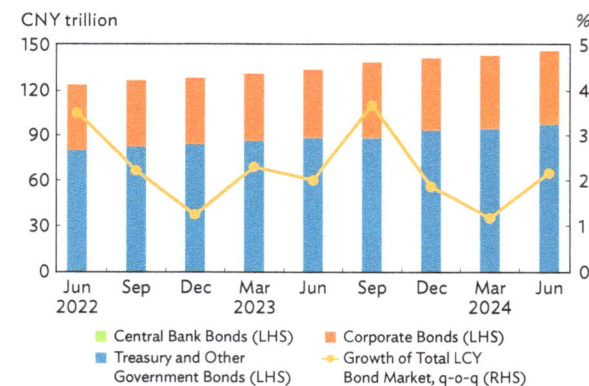

Figure 2: Composition of Local Currency Bonds Outstanding in the People's Republic of China

CNY trillion   %

Central Bank Bonds (LHS)   Corporate Bonds (LHS)
Treasury and Other Government Bonds (LHS)   Growth of Total LCY Bond Market, q-o-q (RHS)

CNY = Chinese yuan, LCY = local currency, LHS = left-hand side, q-o-q = quarter-on-quarter, RHS = right-hand side.
Source: CEIC Data Company.

This market summary was written by Russ Jason Lo, consultant, Economic Research and Development Impact Department, ADB, Manila.

The PRC's LCY bond sales rose to CNY11.7 trillion in Q2 2024 due to robust government bond issuance (Figure 3). Government bond issuance rose 32.2% q-o-q in Q2 2024, after declining 24.4% q-o-q in Q1 2024, as the government began issuing special long-term Treasury bonds to support stimulus measures. While corporate bond issuance also grew in Q2 2024, it expanded at a slower pace compared to government bonds but at a faster rate than in the previous quarter, rising 9.2% as banks issued additional bonds to help shore up regulatory capital.

Figure 3: Composition of Local Currency Bond Issuance in the People's Republic of China

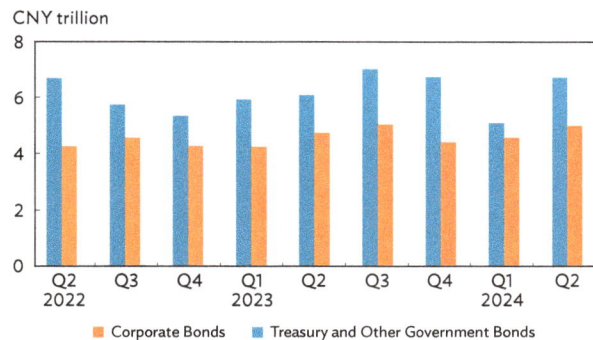

CNY = Chinese yuan, Q1 = first quarter, Q2 = second quarter, Q3 = third quarter, Q4 = fourth quarter.
Source: CEIC Data Company.

Investor Profile

Commercial banks remained the largest holder of Treasury bonds in the PRC at the end of June. Commercial banks shored up their holdings of Treasury bonds following an increase in bond prices, resulting in their holdings share to rising to 70.4% at the end of June from 68.5% a year earlier (**Figure 4**). This led to concerns of an asset bubble in the domestic bond market and, in response, the government sought to limit speculative activities.

Figure 4: Investor Profile of Treasury Bonds

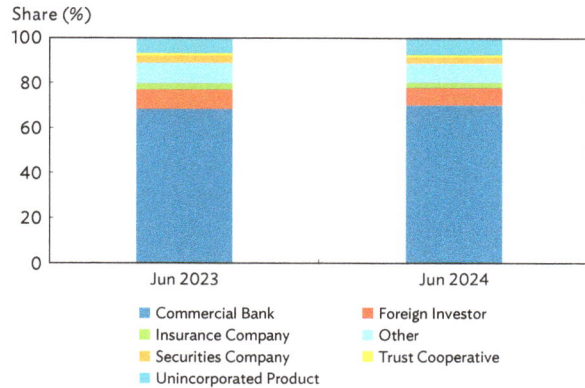

Source: CEIC Data Company.

Sustainable Bond Market

In the PRC, green bonds comprised 90.0% of total outstanding sustainable bonds at the end of June. Corporate bonds comprise the bulk (93.6%) of the PRC's total sustainable bond market (**Figure 5**). Corporate issuers tend to issue shorter-tenors compared to the public sector. As a result, 87.0% of the PRC's outstanding sustainable bonds carried tenors of 5 years or less.

Figure 5: Market Profile of Outstanding Sustainable Bonds in the People's Republic of China at the End of June 2024

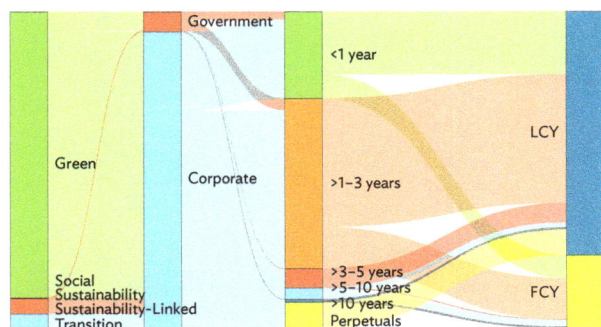

FCY = foreign currency, LCY = local currency.
Source: *AsianBondsOnline* calculations based on Bloomberg LP data.

Hong Kong, China

Yield Movements

Local currency (LCY) government bond yields in Hong Kong, China fell for all tenors between 1 June and 30 August on market expectations of policy easing in the United States (US). Bond yields dropped an average of 86 basis points across all maturities, with the 2-year tenor posting the steepest decline at 110 basis points (**Figure 1**). Softening inflation and weak July employment figures in the US prompted markets to anticipate a rate cut by the Federal Reserve in September, driving down government bond yields globally. The decline in government bond yields was more pronounced in Hong Kong, China compared to its regional peers since the Hong Kong Monetary Authority's monetary policy moves in lockstep with that of the US, owing to the Hong Kong dollar's peg to the US dollar. Domestic inflation in Hong Kong, China remained moderate, but rose to 2.5% year-on-year in July from 1.5% year-on-year in June, largely due to the end of property rate concessions in June.

Local Currency Bond Market Size and Issuance

Hong Kong, China's LCY bonds outstanding posted a nominal 0.4% quarter-on-quarter (q-o-q) contraction in the second quarter (Q2) of 2024 due to a large volume of maturities in government bonds. LCY bonds outstanding totaled HKD3,033.6 billion at the end of June, down from HKD3,045.1 billion at the end of March, as a decline in outstanding Hong Kong Special Administrative Region (HKSAR) government bonds outstripped modest expansions in Exchange Fund Bills and Notes and corporate bonds (**Figure 2**). The stock of HKSAR government bonds fell 9.9% q-o-q due to a relatively large volume of maturities and a contraction in issuance during the quarter. Outstanding Exchange Fund Bills and Notes rose 1.0% q-o-q, while corporate bonds outstanding inched up 0.2% q-o-q. At the end of June, corporate bonds outstanding (HKD1,493.2 billion) comprised nearly half of total LCY bonds, while Exchange Fund Bills and Notes (HKD1,281.7 billion) and HKSAR government bonds (HKD258.7 billion) accounted for the remaining 42.2% and 8.5% shares, respectively.

Figure 1: Hong Kong, China's Benchmark Yield Curve— Local Currency Government Bonds

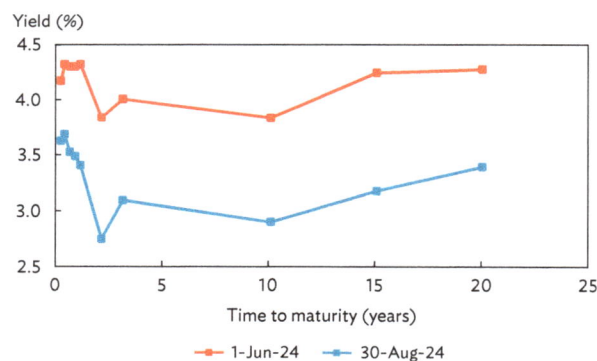

Source: Based on data from Bloomberg LP.

Figure 2: Composition of Local Currency Bonds Outstanding in Hong Kong, China

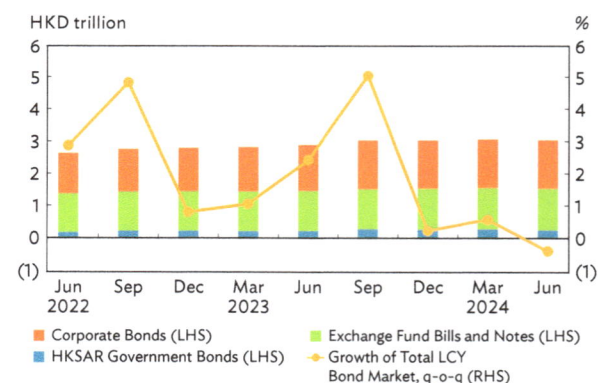

( ) = negative, HKD = Hong Kong dollar, HKSAR = Hong Kong Special Administrative Region, LCY = local currency, LHS = left-hand side, q-o-q = quarter-on-quarter, RHS = right-hand side.
Source: Hong Kong Monetary Authority.

This market summary was written by Debbie Gundaya, consultant, Economic Research and Development Impact Department, ADB, Manila.

LCY bond issuance in Hong Kong, China posted modest growth in Q2 2024, supported solely by increased issuance of Exchange Fund Bills and Notes. Total LCY bond sales amounted to HKD1,275.2 billion in Q2 2024, up 0.4% from the previous quarter (**Figure 3**). Growth was driven by a 1.3% q-o-q rise in Exchange Fund Bills and Notes issuance. Meanwhile, issuance of new HKSAR government bonds contracted 72.7% q-o-q amid plans to gradually replace the existing Government Bond Program with the Infrastructure Bond and Sustainable Bond Programs. Corporate bond sales in Q2 2024 tallied HKD256.4 billion, down 1.3% q-o-q as borrowing costs remained elevated. Hong Kong Mortgage Corporation was the top nonbank corporate issuer during the quarter, with cumulative issuance of HKD11.8 billion that represented 71.7% of total nonbank issuance.

Sustainable Bond Market

At the end of June, sustainable bonds outstanding in Hong Kong, China were predominantly green bond instruments issued by the public sector. Sustainable bonds outstanding totaled USD41.6 billion at the end of Q2 2024, contracting 4.0% q-o-q due to a decline in issuance. Green bonds dominate the sustainable bond market in Hong Kong, China, comprising over 80% of outstanding instruments at the end of June, followed by social bonds with a share of more than 10% (**Figure 4**). Government-issued green bonds comprised nearly two-thirds of outstanding sustainable bonds. Outstanding sustainable bonds are concentrated in short- to medium-term maturities—over 70% of outstanding instruments had remaining maturities of up to 5 years, and the size-weighted average tenor of sustainable bonds outstanding was 4.3 years at the end of June. Over three-quarters of outstanding sustainable bonds at the end of June were denominated in foreign currencies, primarily US dollars. New issuance in Q2 2024 totaled USD385.5 million, comprising green and sustainability-linked instruments issued by the private sector.

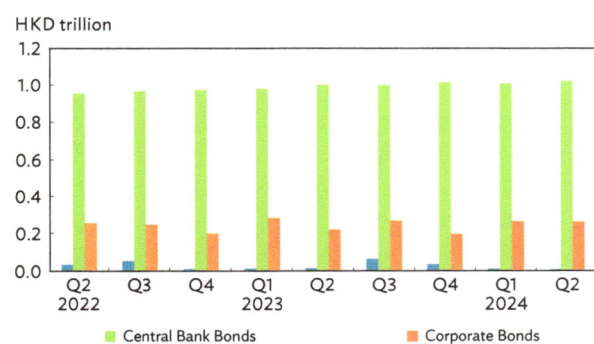

Figure 3: Composition of Local Currency Bond Issuance in Hong Kong, China

HKD trillion

HKD = Hong Kong dollar, Q1 = first quarter, Q2 = second quarter, Q3 = third quarter, Q4 = fourth quarter.
Source: Hong Kong Monetary Authority.

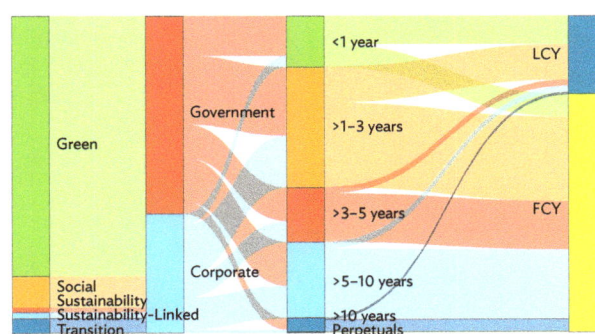

Figure 4: Market Profile of Outstanding Sustainable Bonds in Hong Kong, China at the End of June 2024

FCY = foreign currency, LCY = local currency.
Source: *AsianBondsOnline* calculations based on Bloomberg LP data.

Indonesia

Yield Movements

Between 1 June and 30 August, local currency (LCY) sovereign bond yields in Indonesia fell an average of 25 basis points across the curve, leading the yield curve to shift downward (**Figure 1**). The decline in yields was largely supported by easing inflation and expectations of a policy rate cut by Bank Indonesia. Inflation has ticked down and stayed within the target range of 1.5%–3.5% thus far in 2024. The yield declines were also fueled by expectations of the end of monetary policy tightening by the United States Federal Reserve, which was hinted at the 30–31 July Federal Open Market Committee meeting. Since then, emerging East Asian currencies collectively appreciated against the United States dollar, with the Indonesian rupiah strengthening by 5.1% during the review period.[14]

Figure 2: Composition of Local Currency Bonds Outstanding in Indonesia

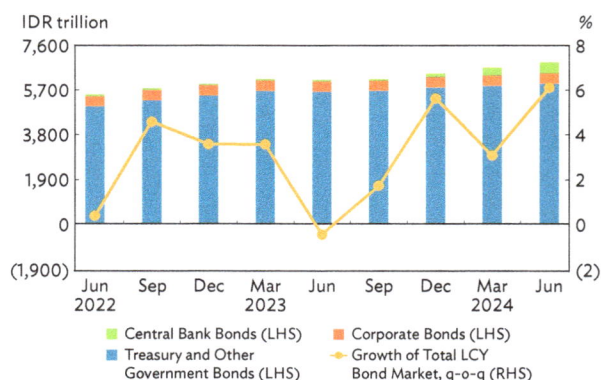

( ) = negative, IDR = Indonesian rupiah, LCY = local currency, LHS = left-hand side, q-o-q = quarter-on-quarter, RHS = right-hand side.
Notes: Data include *sukuk* (Islamic bonds). Data for Treasury and other government bonds comprise tradable and nontradable central government bonds.
Sources: Bank Indonesia; Directorate General of Budget Financing and Risk Management, Ministry of Finance; and Indonesia Stock Exchange.

Local Currency Bond Market Size and Issuance

The LCY bond market in Indonesia recorded a faster quarter-on-quarter (q-o-q) expansion in the second quarter (Q2) of 2024 with all bond types posting positive growth. The outstanding size of the market totaled IDR7,200.3 trillion at the end of June, with growth

Figure 1: Indonesia's Benchmark Yield Curve— Local Currency Government Bonds

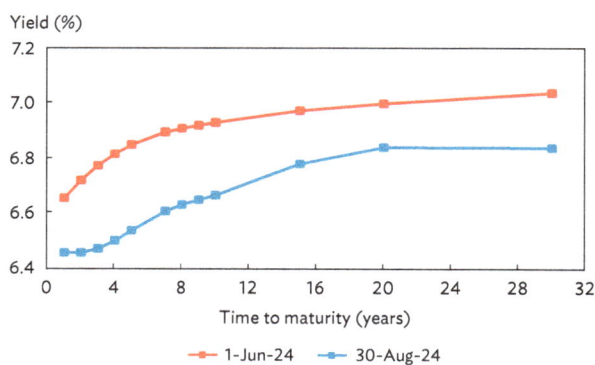

Source: Based on data from Bloomberg LP.

accelerating to 6.1% q-o-q in Q2 2024 from 3.1% q-o-q in the first quarter (**Figure 2**). Central government bonds, which comprised 82.9% of total LCY bonds, grew 1.6% q-o-q despite reduced issuance during the quarter. Corporate bonds accounted for 6.4% of the bond total at the end of Q2 2024, expanding 1.1% q-o-q as issuance picked up. Central bank bonds recorded the fastest q-o-q growth (69.1%) across all bond types. Bank Indonesia continued to optimize issuance of various central bank instruments as part of measures to strengthen monetary operations and attract capital inflows to help stabilize the rupiah.

LCY bond issuance rebounded in Q2 2024, buoyed by robust growth in central bank and corporate bonds. Aggregate issuance reached IDR760.3 trillion in Q2 2024 on growth of 12.3% q-o-q, reversing the 0.6% q-o-q contraction in the previous quarter (**Figure 3**). Central bank bond issuance grew 33.6% q-o-q in Q2 2024, as Bank Indonesia strengthened monetary operations to support the rupiah. Corporate bond issuance also rose 35.8% q-o-q amid declining funding costs, albeit its contribution to total issuance remained

---

This market summary was written by Roselyn Regalado, consultant, Economic Research and Development Impact Department, ADB, Manila.

[14] Emerging East Asia is defined to include member states of the Association of Southeast Asian Nations plus the People's Republic of China; Hong Kong, China; and the Republic of Korea.

Figure 3: Composition of Local Currency Bond Issuance in Indonesia

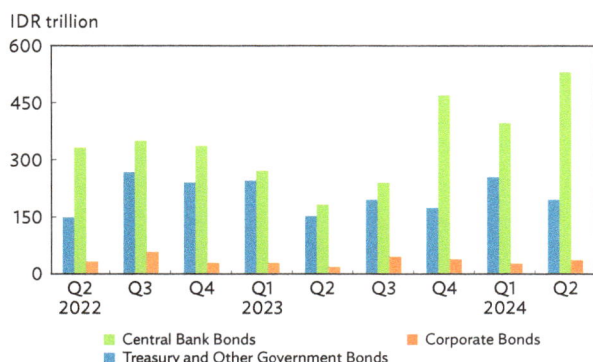

IDR = Indonesian rupiah, Q1 = first quarter, Q2 = second quarter, Q3 = third quarter, Q4 = fourth quarter.

Notes: Data include *sukuk* (Islamic bonds). Data for Treasury and other government bonds comprise tradable and nontradable central government bonds.

Sources: Bank Indonesia; Directorate General of Budget Financing and Risk Management, Ministry of Finance; and Indonesia Stock Exchange.

relatively small (4.5% of the total). Manufacturing firm Indah Kiat Pulp & Paper Mills was the largest corporate bond issuer during the quarter, raising bonds worth IDR4.7 trillion and accounting for 13.5% of the corporate issuance total.

Investor Profile

Domestic investors continued to account for a majority of Indonesia's LCY tradable government bonds with holdings share of 86.1% at the end of June. Among domestic investors, the largest investor group was the central bank, whose collective holdings climbed to 23.1% at the end of June from 17.4% a year earlier, largely due to Bank Indonesia's continued support to ensure bond market stability, particularly during market selloffs when the holdings of foreign investors decline. The Indonesian bond market has the largest share of central bank holdings in emerging East Asia. Bank Indonesia's holdings share of conventional bonds stood at 25.5%, while the corresponding share for Islamic bonds was much lower at 13.1% (**Figure 4**). Insurance and pension funds also increased their bond holdings to an aggregate share of 19.0% at the end of June, up from 17.3% a year earlier.

Sustainable Bond Market

The sustainable bond market of Indonesia is dominated by green bond instruments and long-term financing (Figure 5). Green bonds were the more prevalent sustainable bond type, accounting for 80.0% of the sustainable bond total at the end of June. About 65% of sustainable bond financing was in longer tenors (over 5 years), owing to the strong participation of the public sector. Long-term financing comprised 81.6% of public sector sustainable bonds, while short-term maturities (less than 5 years) were more common for the private sector at a 67.4% share. Indonesia's sustainable bond market had a size-weighted average tenor of 7.3 years at the end of June. Meanwhile, outstanding sustainable bonds in the Indonesian market tallied USD12.4 billion on growth of 3.5% q-o-q in Q2 2024.

Figure 4: Investor Profile of Tradable Central Government Bonds

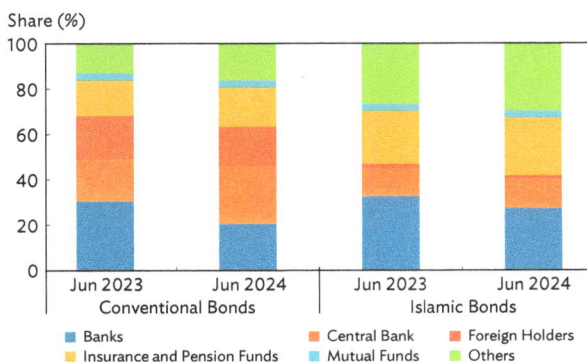

Source: Directorate General of Budget Financing and Risk Management, Ministry of Finance.

Figure 5: Market Profile of Outstanding Sustainable Bonds in Indonesia at the End of June 2024

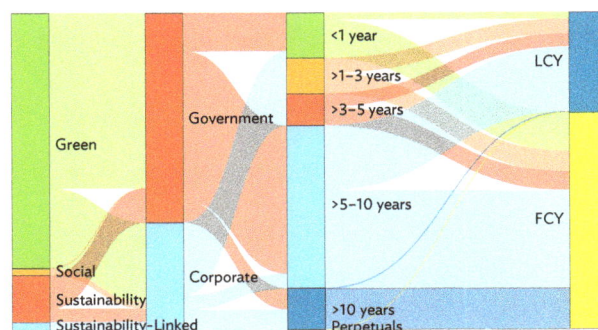

FCY = foreign currency, LCY = local currency.
Source: *AsianBondsOnline* calculations based on Bloomberg LP data.

Republic of Korea

Yield Movements

Local currency (LCY) government bond yields in the Republic of Korea fell for all tenors between 1 June and 30 August, driven by expected rate cuts from the Bank of Korea and the United States Federal Reserve. On average, yields fell 39 basis points during the review period (**Figure 1**). The expectations of a rate cut by the Bank of Korea at its upcoming October meeting—and as market participants priced in a rate cut by the Federal Reserve in its September meeting—pulled down yields. While the Bank of Korea left the base rate unchanged at its 11 July and 22 August meetings, the central bank indicated that the timing of a rate cut depends on the path of inflation and gross domestic product growth, as well as the impact of rising household debt on financial stability. The recent 0.2% quarter-on-quarter (q-o-q) contraction in the Republic of Korea's economy in the second quarter (Q2) of 2024 also contributed to market participants pricing in a rate cut in October. Furthermore, in its 22 August meeting, the Bank of Korea lowered its 2024 economic growth and inflation forecasts by 0.1 percentage point each to 2.4% year-on-year and 2.5% y-o-y, respectively, from its May forecasts.

Figure 1: The Republic of Korea's Benchmark Yield Curve—Local Currency Government Bonds

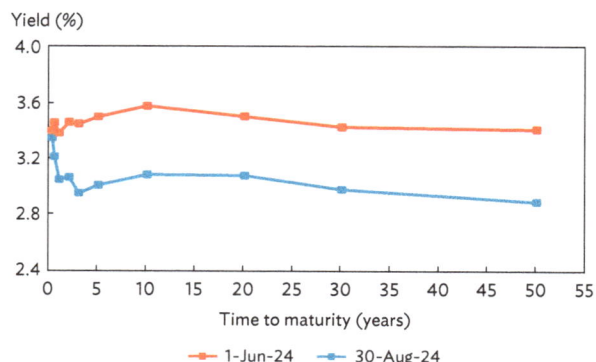

Source: Based on data from Bloomberg LP.

Local Currency Bond Market Size and Issuance

The Republic of Korea's LCY bonds outstanding grew at a faster pace in Q2 2024 as the stock of both government and corporate bonds increased during the quarter. The size of the Republic of Korea's LCY bond market rose 3.9% q-o-q to reach KRW3,398.3 trillion at the end of June (**Figure 2**). The Republic of Korea's government bond market increased 2.7% q-o-q in Q2 2024 due to higher quarterly issuance of Treasury bonds. Meanwhile, corporate bonds outstanding grew 5.0% q-o-q because of the smaller volume of maturities, despite a contraction in issuance.

Figure 2: Composition of Local Currency Bonds Outstanding in the Republic of Korea

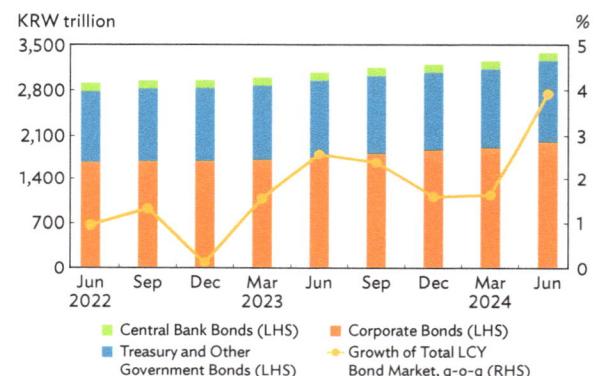

KRW = Korean won, LCY = local currency, LHS = left-hand side, q-o-q = quarter-on-quarter, RHS = right-hand side.
Sources: Bank of Korea and KG Zeroin Corp.

LCY bond issuance fell 6.8% q-o-q to KRW242.0 trillion in Q2 2024, driven by a contraction in the corporate bond segment. Corporate bond issuance dropped 13.9% q-o-q in Q2 2024 due to lower corporate funding requirements amid a slowdown in domestic and global economic growth. Meanwhile, issuance of government bonds rose 15.4% q-o-q in Q2 2024, which was still in line with the government's frontloading policy in the first half of the year (**Figure 3**).

This market summary was written by Angelica Andrea Cruz, consultant, Economic Research and Development Impact Department, ADB, Manila.

Figure 3: Composition of Local Currency Bond Issuance in the Republic of Korea

KRW trillion

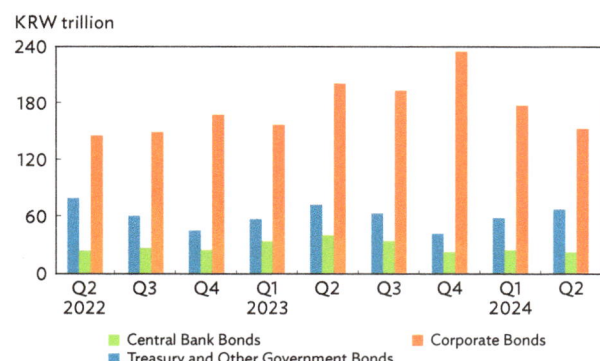

KRW = Korean won, Q1 = first quarter, Q2 = second quarter, Q3 = third quarter, Q4 = fourth quarter.

Sources: Bank of Korea and KG Zeroin Corp.

Investor Profile

The Republic of Korea's LCY government bond market continued to have one of the most diverse investor bases in emerging East Asia at the end of March.[15] The Republic of Korea had the second-lowest Herfindahl–Hirschman Index score in the region at the end of March.[16] Insurance companies and pension funds remained the largest investor group in the LCY government

bond market with a share of 29.0%; followed by banks and foreign investors with shares of 20.7% and 19.2%, respectively (**Figure 4**). Meanwhile, the corporate bond market has a less diverse investor base and is largely held by two major investor groups. Other financial institutions held a share of 41.1%, followed by insurance companies and pension funds at 29.4%. Foreign holdings of the LCY corporate bond market remained negligible at the end of March.

Sustainable Bond Market

Sustainable bonds outstanding in the Republic of Korea at the end of June were mostly social bonds and carried tenors of 3 years or less. The Republic of Korea was the second-largest sustainable bond market in the region with outstanding bonds worth USD177.6 billion at the end of June on marginal contraction of 1.3% q-o-q. Social bonds comprised 50.8% of the sustainable bond market, of which the majority were issued by the government (**Figure 5**). This was followed by green bonds at 30.7%, mostly coming from the private sector. Almost 70% of the sustainable bonds outstanding carried maturities of less than 3 years, resulting in an overall size-weighted average tenor of 3.1 years. In terms of currency denomination, about 60% of sustainable bonds outstanding at the end of June were denominated in Korean won.

Figure 4: Local Currency Bonds Outstanding Investor Profile

%

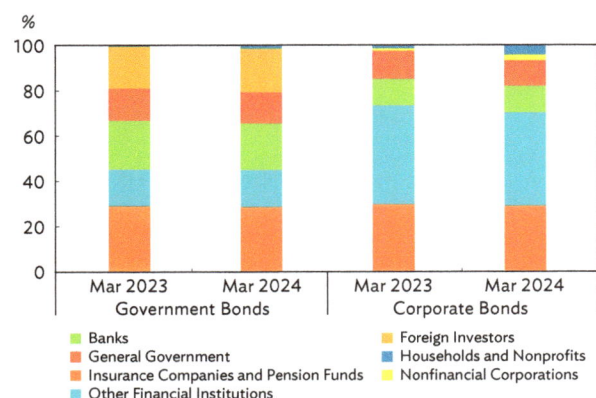

Sources: *AsianBondsOnline* and Bank of Korea.

Figure 5: Market Profile of Outstanding Sustainable Bonds in the Republic of Korea at the End of June 2024

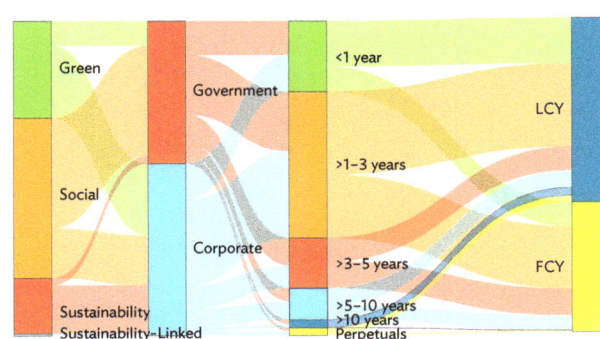

FCY = foreign currency, LCY = local currency.

Source: *AsianBondsOnline* calculations based on Bloomberg LP data.

---

[15] Emerging East Asia is defined to include member states of the Association of Southeast Asian Nations plus the People's Republic of China; Hong Kong, China; and the Republic of Korea

[16] The Herfindahl–Hirschman Index is a common measure of market concentration. The index is used to measure the investor profile diversification of the local currency bond market by summing the squared share of each investor group in the bond market.

Malaysia

Yield Movements

Local currency (LCY) government bond yields in Malaysia fell for all tenors between 1 June and 30 August on expectations of policy rate cuts by the United States Federal Reserve. Yields fell an average of 14 basis points across the curve during the review period (**Figure 1**). Yields fell on increased expectations of a policy rate cut by the Federal Reserve in its September meeting amid moderating inflation and weak labor data. The drop in yields was further supported by continued foreign bond inflows in the domestic bond market. With Bank Negara Malaysia expected to maintain its policy rate for the rest of the year, domestic bonds are deemed even more attractive by investors as the Federal Reserve signals impending rate cuts. On 11 July, Bank Negara Malaysia held its policy rate steady at 3.50% amid stable inflation and sustained economic growth.

Local Currency Bond Market Size and Issuance

Growth in Malaysia's LCY bonds outstanding moderated in the second quarter (Q2) of 2024 amid reduced issuance of central bank bills. The LCY bond market reached a size of MYR2.1 trillion at the end of June on 0.9% quarter-on-quarter (q-o-q) growth, supported by both the government and corporate bond segments. However, the reduced stock of central bank bills led to a slowdown in overall growth (**Figure 2**). Government bond market grew 1.6% q-o-q in Q2 2024, driven by increased issuance of Treasury bills. Meanwhile, corporate bonds outstanding rose 1.3% q-o-q in Q2 2024 due to a rebound in issuance during the quarter. *Sukuk* (Islamic bonds) continued to comprise a majority of the total LCY bond market in Q2 2024 with a share of 63.4% at the end of June.

Figure 1: Malaysia's Benchmark Yield Curve— Local Currency Government Bonds

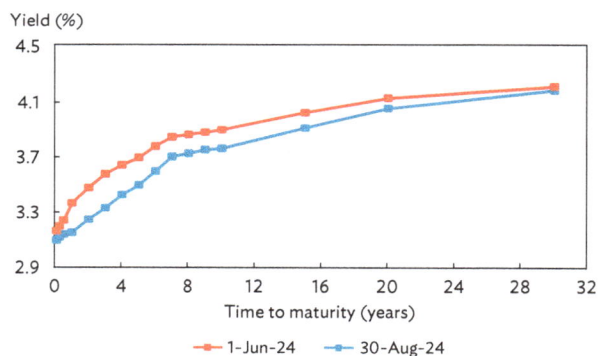

Source: Based on data from Bloomberg LP.

Figure 2: Composition of Local Currency Bonds Outstanding in Malaysia

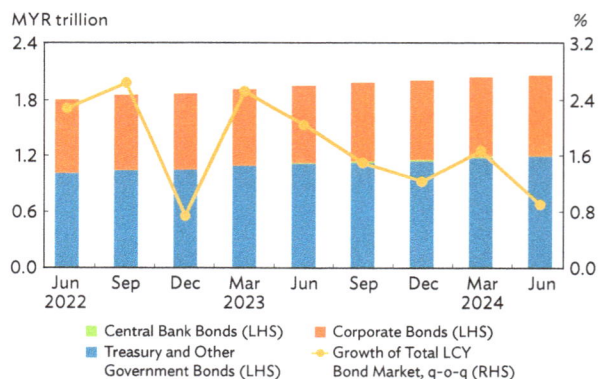

LCY = local currency, LHS = left-hand side, MYR = Malaysian ringgit, q-o-q = quarter-on-quarter, RHS = right-hand side.
Source: Bank Negara Malaysia Fully Automated System for Issuing/Tendering.

This market summary was written by Angelica Andrea Cruz, consultant, Economic Research and Development Impact Department, ADB, Manila.

Total LCY bond issuance in Malaysia was dragged down by a contraction in issuance of central bank bills. In 2023, Bank Negara Malaysia increased its issuance of central bank bills as part of efforts to manage excess liquidity in the market. However, the central bank curtailed its issuance starting in the first quarter of 2024 as liquidity conditions stabilized (**Figure 3**). Meanwhile, issuance of government bonds rose 25.0% q-o-q in Q2 2024, primarily due to higher issuance of Treasury bills. Corporate bond issuances also increased 17.1% q-o-q, as companies took advantage of lower borrowing costs amid declining bond yields. Despite these increases, LCY bond issuance fell 13.6% q-o-q to MYR116.4 billion in Q2 2024, again largely due to the reduction in central bank bill issuance.

Investor Profile

Bond holdings in Malaysia remained unchanged from a year earlier. Nearly 80% of Malaysia's LCY government bonds outstanding were held by domestic investors at the end of March. Among these domestic investors, financial institutions and social security institutions held the largest shares at 33.2% and 29.8%, respectively (**Figure 4**). Meanwhile, foreign holdings in Malaysia's domestic government bond market slightly decreased to 21.2% at the end of March from 22.7% a year earlier.

Sustainable Bond Market

At the end of June, Malaysia's sustainable bond market largely comprised long-term sustainability bonds issued by the corporate sector. The size of Malaysia's sustainable bond market reached USD14.2 billion at the end of June on 3.5% q-o-q growth. Sustainability bonds comprised almost three-fourths of the sustainable bond market, with green bonds the next most common bond type (**Figure 5**). A majority of sustainable bonds outstanding at the end of June were issued by private corporations and carried maturities of more than 5 years. Sustainable bonds issued by the government were also only longer-term securities. Consequently, the size-weighted average tenor of sustainable bonds in Malaysia at the end of June was 8.7 years. Over 80% of the sustainable bonds outstanding in Malaysia at the end of Q2 2024 were denominated in ringgit.

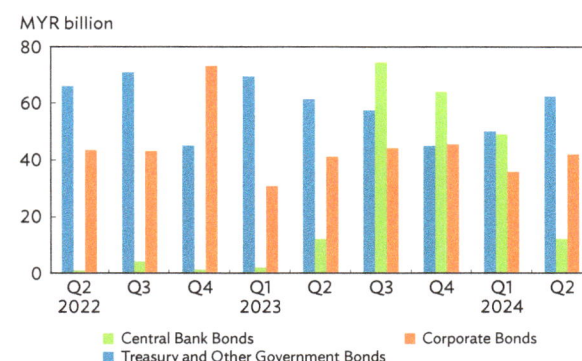

Figure 3: Composition of Local Currency Bond Issuance in Malaysia

MYR = Malaysian ringgit, Q1 = first quarter, Q2 = second quarter, Q3 = third quarter, Q4 = fourth quarter.
Source: Bank Negara Malaysia Fully Automated System for Issuing/Tendering.

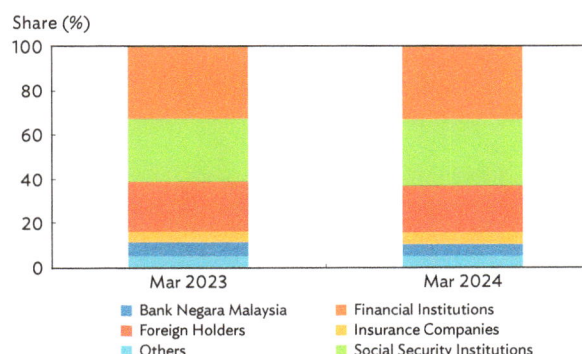

Figure 4: Local Currency Government Bonds Investor Profile

Note: "Others" include statutory bodies, nominees and trustee companies, and cooperatives and unclassified items.
Source: Bank Negara Malaysia.

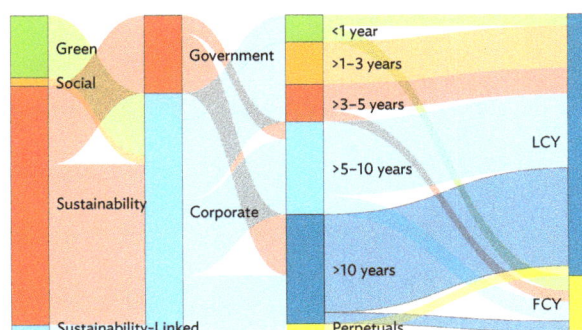

Figure 5: Market Profile of Outstanding Sustainable Bonds in Malaysia at the End of June 2024

FCY = foreign currency, LCY = local currency.
Source: *AsianBondsOnline* calculations based on Bloomberg LP data.

Philippines

Yield Movements

Between 1 June and 30 August, local currency (LCY) government bond yields in the Philippines declined across most tenors. Yields fell by an average of 52 basis points for tenors of 2 years and longer, largely driven by the Bangko Sentral ng Pilipinas' (BSP) monetary policy easing (**Figure 1**). On 15 August, the BSP reduced its overnight reverse repurchase rate by 25 basis points to 6.25%, citing that inflation was consistent with its target path and is expected to trend downward for the rest of 2024. Year-on-year inflation slowed to 3.3% in August from 4.4% in July, settling within the government's target range of 2.0%–4.0%. Rising expectations of a policy rate cut by the United States Federal Reserve also contributed to the fall in domestic yields during the review period.

Local Currency Bond Market Size and Issuance

In the second quarter (Q2) of 2024, LCY bond market growth moderated on reduced issuance from both the corporate and government segments. Total LCY bonds outstanding reached PHP12.5 trillion at the end of June, with growth moderating to 1.9% quarter-on-quarter (q-o-q) from 2.2% q-o-q in the previous quarter (**Figure 2**). Treasury and other government bonds increased 2.8% q-o-q due to a lower volume of bond maturities during the quarter. Conversely, the total corporate debt stock contracted 7.7% q-o-q in Q2 2024, following the previous quarter's 8.2% q-o-q decline.

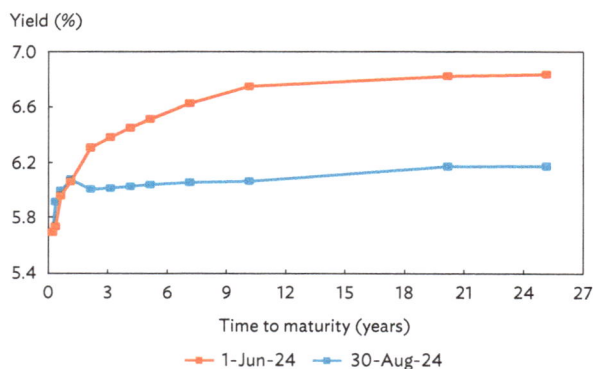

Figure 1: The Philippines' Benchmark Yield Curve—Local Currency Government Bonds

Source: Based on data from Bloomberg LP.

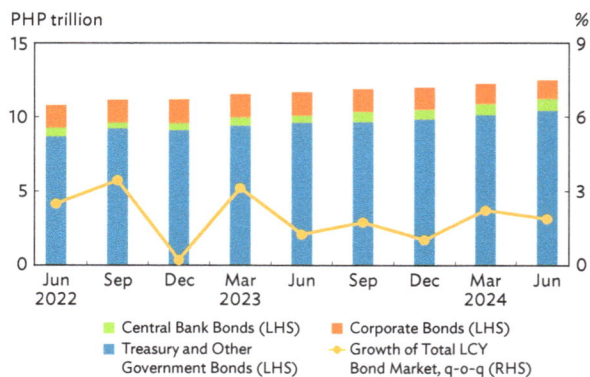

Figure 2: Composition of Local Currency Bonds Outstanding in the Philippines

LCY = local currency, LHS = left-hand side, PHP = Philippine peso, q-o-q = quarter-on-quarter, RHS = right-hand side.

Note: Treasury and other government bonds comprise Treasury bonds, Treasury bills, and bonds issued by government agencies, entities, and corporations for which repayment is guaranteed by the Government of the Philippines. This includes bonds issued by Power Sector Assets and Liabilities Management and the National Food Authority, among others.

Sources: Bureau of the Treasury and Bloomberg LP.

This market summary was written by Jeremy Grace Ilustrisimo, consultant, Economic Research and Development Impact Department, ADB, Manila.

Bond issuances contracted in Q2 2024 amid high interest rates. Total LCY bond issuance contracted 15.7% q-o-q to PHP2.6 trillion in Q2 2024, a reversal from the previous quarter's 37.3% q-o-q expansion (**Figure 3**). Issuance of Treasury and other government bonds declined 51.7% q-o-q in Q2 2024 mainly due to the exceptionally high issuance volume in the previous quarter, driven by the sale of Retail Treasury bonds in February. Similarly, corporate bond issuance fell 41.2% q-o-q amid persistently elevated interest rates as corporates postponed bond issuances in anticipation of an interest rate cut from the BSP in August. The largest corporate bond issuances during the quarter came from SM Prime Holdings and Energy Development Corporation, which accounted for 58.0% and 23.2%, respectively, of the Q2 2024 corporate issuance total.

Figure 3: Composition of Local Currency Bond Issuance in the Philippines

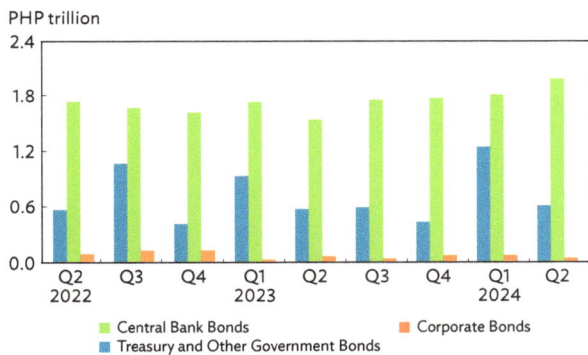

PHP = Philippine peso, Q1 = first quarter, Q2 = second quarter, Q3 = third quarter, Q4 = fourth quarter.

Note: Treasury and other government bonds comprise Treasury bonds, Treasury bills, and bonds issued by government agencies, entities, and corporations for which repayment is guaranteed by the Government of the Philippines. This includes bonds issued by Power Sector Assets and Liabilities Management and the National Food Authority, among others.

Sources: Bureau of the Treasury and Bloomberg LP.

Investor Profile

The investor landscape of the LCY government bond market at the end of June was largely unchanged from a year earlier. Banks and investment houses continued to be the largest investor group, holding nearly 50% of the total LCY government debt stock at the end of June (**Figure 4**). This was followed by contractual savings institutions and tax-exempt institutions with investment holdings dipping to 30.9% from 31.8% from the previous year.

Figure 4: Investor Profile of Local Currency Government Bonds

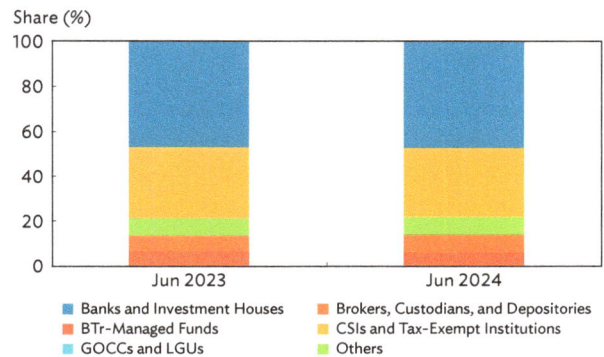

BTr = Bureau of the Treasury, CSI = contractual savings institution, GOCC = government-owned or -controlled corporation, LGU = local government unit.

Note: At the end of June, the aggregate holdings share for government-owned or -controlled corporations and local government units was 0.02%, amounting to PHP2.2 billion.

Source: Bureau of the Treasury.

Sustainable Bond Market

At the end of June, foreign-currency-denominated sustainability bond instruments dominated the sustainable bond market in the Philippines. Sustainability bond instruments comprised 77.0% of the total sustainable bonds at the end of June (**Figure 5**). The total size of sustainable bond market reached USD9.0 billion in Q2 2024, with the government and corporate segments each comprising a roughly equal share of the market. The government sector tends to issue longer tenors that are denominated in foreign currencies, while the private sector is inclined to issue sustainable bonds with tenors of less than 10 years. At the end of June, the size-weighted average tenor in the Philippines' sustainable bond market was 12.7 years.

Figure 5: Market Profile of Outstanding Sustainable Bonds in the Philippines at the End of June 2024

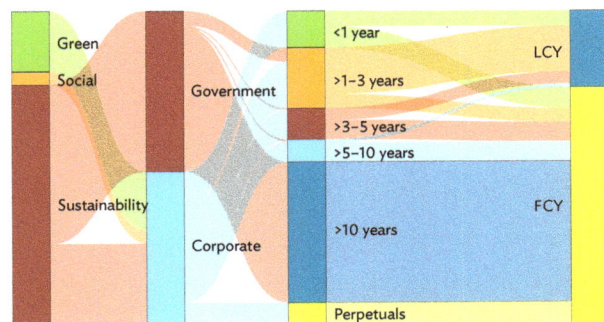

FCY = foreign currency, LCY = local currency.

Source: *AsianBondsOnline* calculations based on Bloomberg LP data.

Singapore

Yield Movements

Local currency (LCY) government bond yields in Singapore declined for all tenors between 1 June and 30 August, largely tracking the yield curve movements of United States Treasuries. Yields declined by an average of 57 basis points on increased expectations of a policy rate cut by the United States Federal Reserve in September and easing domestic inflation (**Figure 1**). On 26 July, the Monetary Authority of Singapore kept its monetary policy stance unchanged and maintained the rate of appreciation of the Singapore dollar's nominal effective exchange rate, citing sustained positive economic growth prospects and easing inflation. Consumer price inflation in July remained unchanged at 2.4% year-on-year from June, slower than 3.1% year-on-year inflation in May.

Local Currency Bond Market Size and Issuance

Growth in the LCY bond market accelerated in the second quarter (Q2) of 2024, supported by robust expansion in all bond segments. Outstanding LCY bonds grew 5.5% quarter-on-quarter (q-o-q) to SGD775.2 billion, faster than the previous quarter's 2.7% q-o-q increase (**Figure 2**). Treasury and other government bonds posted the largest q-o-q growth (7.2%) among all bond instrument types due to a high volume of issuance and relatively few bonds maturing during the quarter. Growth in the corporate bond segment also accelerated to 4.3% q-o-q in Q2 2024 from 1.6% q-o-q in the first quarter, while central bank securities grew at a steady pace of 4.7% q-o-q.

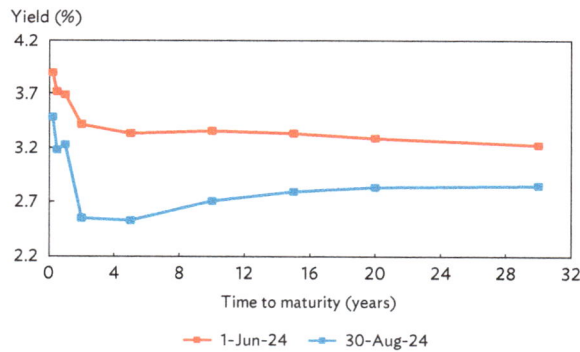

Figure 1: Singapore's Benchmark Yield Curve— Local Currency Government Bonds

Source: Based on data from Bloomberg LP.

Figure 2: Composition of Local Currency Bonds Outstanding in Singapore

LCY = local currency, LHS = left-hand side, q-o-q = quarter-on-quarter, RHS = right-hand side, SGD = Singapore dollar.
Note: Corporate bonds are based on *AsianBondsOnline* estimates.
Sources: Monetary Authority of Singapore and Bloomberg LP.

This market summary was written by Jeremy Grace Ilustrisimo, consultant, Economic Research and Development Impact Department, ADB, Manila.

LCY bond issuance rebounded strongly in Q2 2024 amid market optimism on the domestic economic outlook. Total LCY bond issuance grew 23.2% q-o-q, reversing the preceding quarter's 1.1% q-o-q decline (**Figure 3**). The issuance of Monetary Authority of Singapore bills bounced back from a 2.6% q-o-q decline in the first quarter of 2024 to 22.8% q-o-q growth in Q2 2024. Issuance of Treasury and other government bonds and corporate bonds also posted q-o-q growth of 27.3% and 17.7%, respectively, during the quarter. The Housing & Development Board—a state-owned real estate company—was the largest issuer of corporate bonds in Q2 2024, with the sale of two fixed-income securities totaling SGD1.7 billion, comprising 36.8% of the total corporate issuance during the quarter.

Sustainable Bond Market

At the end of June, the sustainable bond market in Singapore was dominated by government and corporate green bond instruments. Green bonds accounted for 81.0% of the economy's total sustainable debt stock at the end of Q2 2024, mostly denominated in local currency and carrying a tenor of over 5 years (**Figure 4**). Total outstanding sustainable bonds reached USD22.0 billion at the end of June, almost half of which were green bonds issued by the government, while corporate issuances accounted for 53.1%, a majority of which were green bond instruments. At the end of June, over 40.0% of total sustainable bonds outstanding carried a tenor of more than 10 years, resulting in a size-weighted average tenor of 16.7 years. LCY-denominated instruments accounted for about 78.0% of the total. The Government of Singapore had the single-largest issuance during the quarter: a 30-year green bond amounting to USD1.9 billion.

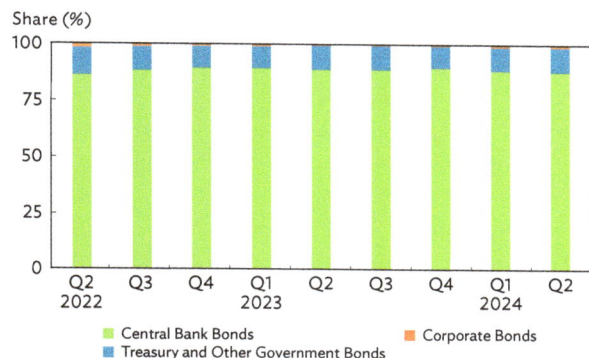

Figure 3: Composition of Local Currency Bond Issuance in Singapore

Q1 = first quarter, Q2 = second quarter, Q3 = third quarter, Q4 = fourth quarter.
Note: Corporate bonds are based on *AsianBondsOnline* estimates.
Sources: Monetary Authority of Singapore and Bloomberg LP.

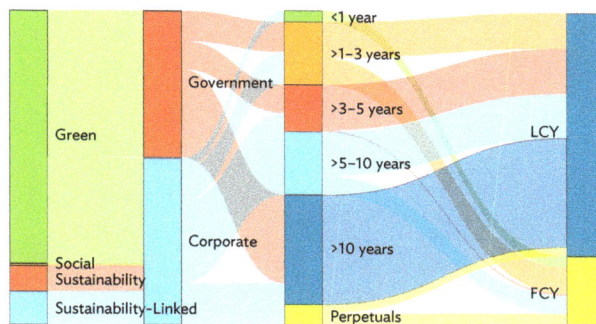

Figure 4: Market Profile of Outstanding Sustainable Bonds in Singapore at the End of June 2024

FCY = foreign currency, LCY = local currency.
Source: *AsianBondsOnline* calculations based on Bloomberg LP data.

Thailand

Yield Movements

Between 1 June and 30 August, local currency (LCY) government bond yields in Thailand fell for all maturities amid heightened expectations of monetary policy easing in the United States (US). Yields fell an average of 20 basis points across all tenors during the review period (**Figure 1**). The decline in yields followed trends in US Treasuries and other regional government bond yields, as markets priced in a rate cut by the Federal Reserve at its forthcoming September meeting amid slowing inflation and weak employment data in the US. Meanwhile, the Bank of Thailand (BOT) held its policy rate steady for a fifth straight meeting on 21 August, stating that the current rate was consistent with the economy's growth potential. Thailand's consumer price inflation eased to 0.4% year-on-year in August from 0.8% year-on-year in July. The BOT expects inflation to rise to its target range of 1.0%–3.0% by the end of 2024.

Figure 1: Thailand's Benchmark Yield Curve— Local Currency Government Bonds

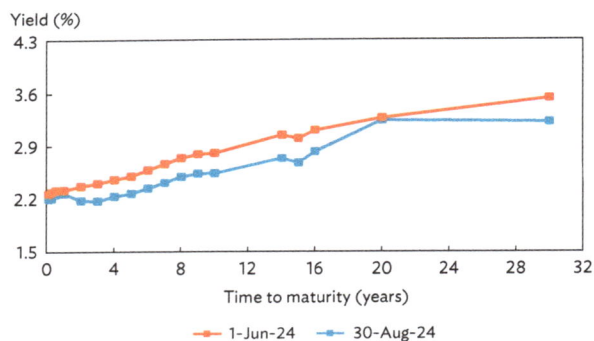

Sources: Based on data from Bloomberg LP and Thai Bond Market Association.

Local Currency Bond Market Size and Issuance

Thailand's LCY bond market posted a nominal contraction in the second quarter (Q2) of 2024 due to declines in the stocks of BOT bonds and corporate bonds. LCY bonds outstanding fell 0.2% quarter-on-

Figure 2: Composition of Local Currency Bonds Outstanding in Thailand

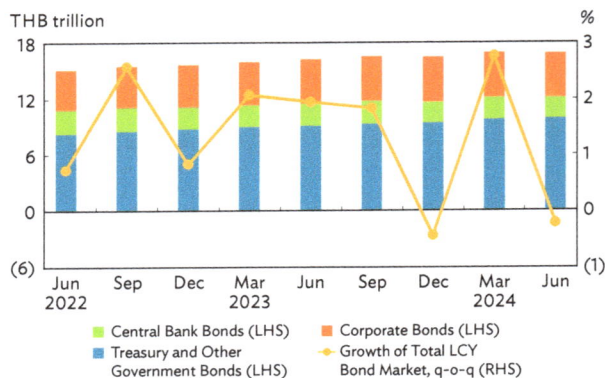

( ) = negative, LCY = local currency, LHS = left-hand side, q-o-q = quarter-on-quarter, RHS = right-hand side, THB = Thai baht.
Source: Bank of Thailand.

quarter (q-o-q) in Q2 2024, amounting to THB16.9 trillion at the end of June (**Figure 2**). Treasury and other government bonds outstanding rose 1.1% q-o-q to THB9.9 trillion, supported by increased issuance as the delayed fiscal year 2024 budget came into effect in April. Meanwhile, outstanding BOT bonds fell 5.3% q-o-q to THB2.2 trillion due to a contraction in issuance. The stock of corporate bonds inched down 0.4% q-o-q to THB4.8 trillion despite a rebound in issuance, owing to a high volume of maturities. Treasury and other government bonds continued to comprise a majority (58.5%) of Thailand's LCY bond market at the end of June.

Thailand's LCY bond issuance gained pace in Q2 2024, supported by increased issuance of Treasury and corporate bonds. Issuance of LCY bonds tallied THB2.3 trillion in Q2 2024, rising 3.5% q-o-q (**Figure 3**). Treasury and other government bond issuance rose 9.1% q-o-q to THB677.1 billion, as the government continued to accelerate debt issuance to fund its budget deficit. Corporate bond issuance rebounded to THB497.2 billion in Q2 2024, expanding 21.1% q-o-q after a 10.3% q-o-q contraction in the previous quarter. Improving economic conditions fueled by a revival of tourism and domestic demand boosted investor confidence, leading to increased corporate debt sales in

This market summary was written by Debbie Gundaya, consultant, Economic Research and Development Impact Department, ADB, Manila.

Figure 3: Composition of Local Currency Bond Issuance in Thailand

THB trillion

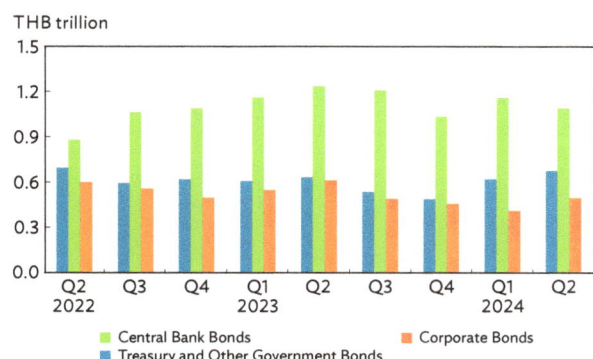

Q1 = first quarter, Q2 = second quarter, Q3 = third quarter, Q4 = fourth quarter, THB = Thai baht.
Source: Bank of Thailand.

Q2 2024. Siam Commercial Bank was the top corporate bond issuer in Q2 2024 with cumulative issuance of THB42.0 billion (8.4% of total corporate issuance). Siam Cement and Gulf Energy Development were the next largest issuers, each with cumulative issuance of THB20.0 billion (4.0% of total corporate issuance).

Investor Profile

Domestic investors held over 90% of Thailand's government bonds at the end of June. Domestic holders' share of LCY government bonds rose to 90.4%

at the end of June from 88.4% a year earlier (**Figure 4**). The increase was largely driven by increased holdings among banks, which rose to a 21.4% share in June from 18.0% in the prior year. In contrast, foreign investors' holdings of Thai sovereign bonds fell to 9.6% from 11.6% during the same period, as interest rates differentials between US Treasury bonds and Thai sovereign bonds remained high.

Sustainable Bond Market

A majority of Thailand's outstanding sustainable bonds are sustainability bonds issued by the government. At the end of June, total sustainable bonds outstanding tallied USD21.1 billion (**Figure 5**). Sustainability bonds comprised a majority of outstanding sustainable bonds (67.6%), followed by green bonds (21.2%). Government-issued instruments accounted for over 70% of outstanding sustainable bonds. Thailand's sustainable bonds outstanding are primarily long-term instruments denominated in baht. At the end of June, the size-weighted average tenor of outstanding sustainable bonds was 9.3 years, among the longest in emerging East Asia.[17] Over 65% of outstanding sustainable bonds had remaining maturities over 10 years, while over 99% of outstanding sustainable bonds were denominated in Thai baht. In Q2 2024, issuance of sustainable bonds amounted to USD244.8 million worth of sustainability and green bonds.

Figure 4: Investor Profile of Government Bonds in Thailand

Share (%)

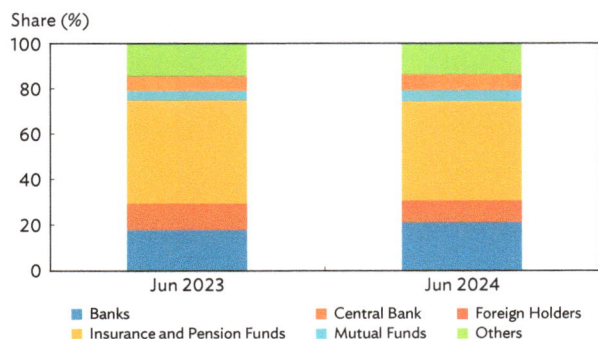

Source: Bank of Thailand.

Figure 5: Market Profile of Outstanding Sustainable Bonds in Thailand at the End of June 2024

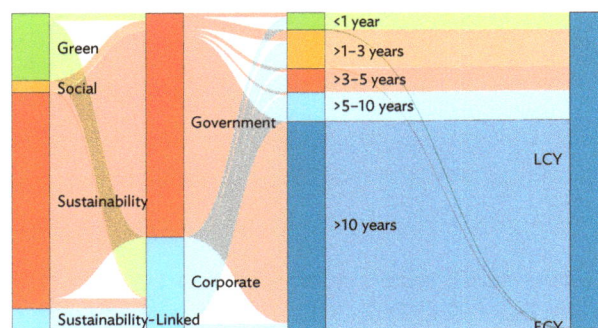

FCY = foreign currency, LCY = local currency.
Source: *AsianBondsOnline* calculations based on Bloomberg LP data.

[17] Emerging East Asia is defined to include member states of the Association of Southeast Asian Nations plus the People's Republic of China; Hong Kong, China; and the Republic of Korea.

Viet Nam

Yield Movements

Between 1 June and 30 August, local currency (LCY) government bond yields in Viet Nam declined for most tenors. Yields decreased by an average of 6 basis points, with the 10-year tenor posting the largest decline of 13 basis points (**Figure 1**). The decline in yields was influenced by heightened expectations of a policy rate cut by the United States Federal Reserve in September, as signaled in its Federal Open Market Committee meeting on 30–31 July. Furthermore, to support liquidity in the economy, the State Bank of Vietnam, on 28 August, reduced the interest rate on central bank bills for the third time in August to 4.15%. Previously, the central bank cut the bills' interest rate from 4.50% to 4.25% on 5 August and was then further reduced to 4.20% on 20 August.

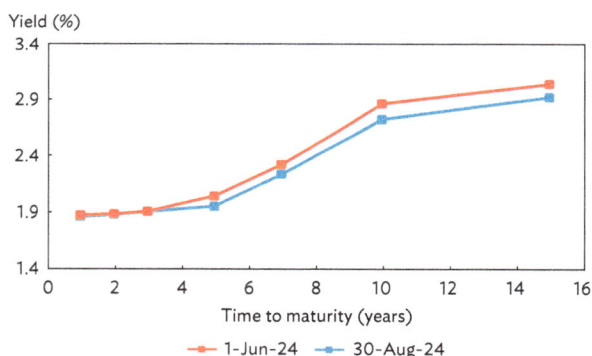

Figure 2: Composition of Local Currency Bonds Outstanding in Viet Nam

( ) = negative, LCY = local currency, LHS = left-hand side, q-o-q = quarter-on-quarter, RHS = right-hand side, VND = Vietnamese dong.
Note: Other government bonds comprise government-guaranteed and municipal bonds.
Sources: Vietnam Bond Market Association and Bloomberg LP.

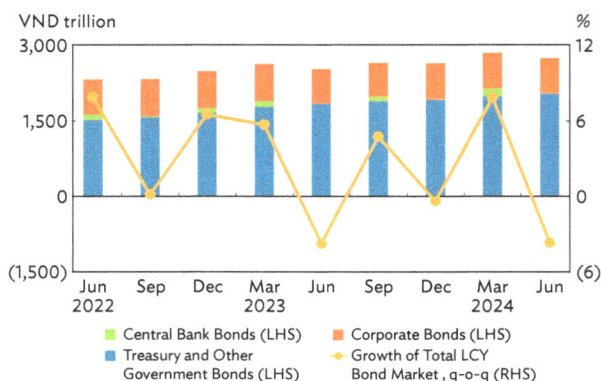

Figure 1: Viet Nam's Benchmark Yield Curve—Local Currency Government Bonds

Source: Based on data from Bloomberg LP.

Local Currency Bond Market Size and Issuance

Viet Nam's LCY bond market contracted in the second quarter (Q2) of 2024 on a high volume of maturities during the quarter. Total outstanding LCY bonds dropped 3.7% quarter-on-quarter (q-o-q) in Q2 2024, mainly driven by a large amount of maturities

for corporate bonds and central bank securities, which outpaced total issuance during the quarter (**Figure 2**). Due to the large amount of corporate bond maturities, the total corporate debt stock dipped 0.8% q-o-q even with increased issuance during the quarter. In contrast, despite weak issuance, outstanding Treasury and other government bonds grew 2.2% q-o-q in Q2 2024 due to a small volume of maturing bonds.

LCY bond issuance declined 29.4% q-o-q in Q2 2024 on tepid issuance from the government and central bank. Issuance of Treasury and other government bonds contracted 33.8% q-o-q, reversing the first quarter's 136.9% q-o-q growth, due to several auctions not being fully awarded during the quarter as investors sought higher rates (**Figure 3**). Central bank securities issuance declined 67.7% q-o-q amid tightened liquidity due to elevated interest rates in the interbank market. Conversely, issuance of corporate bonds in Q2 2024 grew more than four-fold from VND17.6 trillion in the preceding quarter. The increase was mainly driven by the banking sector, as financial institutions raised capital to accelerate credit growth and ensure compliance with the prescribed safety ratios of the State Bank of Vietnam. The

This market summary was written by Jeremy Grace Ilustrisimo, consultant, Economic Research and Development Impact Department, ADB, Manila.

Figure 3: Composition of Local Currency Bond Issuance in Viet Nam

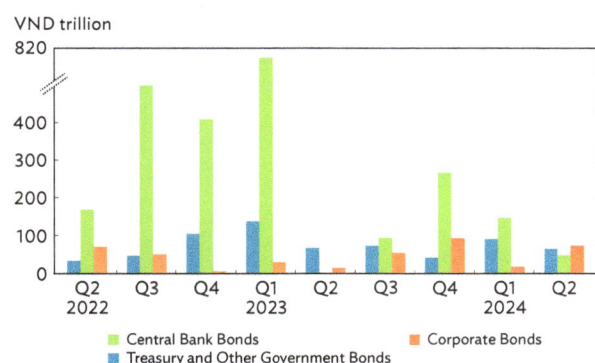

VND trillion

Q1 = first quarter, Q2 = second quarter, Q3 = third quarter, Q4 = fourth quarter, VND = Vietnamese dong.
Note: Other government bonds comprise government-guaranteed and municipal bonds.
Sources: Vietnam Bond Market Association and Bloomberg LP.

property sector was the second-largest issuer of corporate bonds in Q2 2024, as property companies sought funding for debt restructuring after the central bank extended its policy on debt rescheduling until the end of 2024 amid the rising level of bad debts.

Investor Profile

Insurance companies and banks collectively held 99.5% of outstanding government bonds at the end of March. Viet Nam's LCY government bond market had the least diversified investor profile in the region as bond holdings was highly concentrated in these two investor groups only (**Figure 4**). Insurance companies, whose holdings

Figure 4: Profile of the Two Dominant Investors for Local Currency Government Bonds

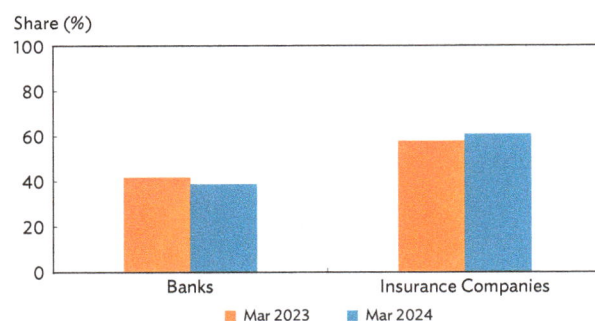

Share (%)

Source: Viet Nam Ministry of Finance.

share increased to 60.8% in March from 57.8% a year earlier, remained the single-largest investor group. This was followed by banks, whose holdings share decreased to 38.7% from 41.7% during the same period.

Sustainable Bond Market

At the end of June, the corporate sector remained the sole issuer of sustainable bonds in Viet Nam. The economy's sustainable bond market comprised green and sustainability bond instruments in Q2 2024, most of which were foreign-currency-denominated and carrying tenors of 1–3 years (**Figure 5**). The total stock of sustainable bonds at the end of Q2 2024 remained at USD0.8 billion, more than half of which comprised sustainability bonds, while the remaining 46.9% were green bonds. Over 78.0% of total sustainable bonds outstanding at the end of June were denominated in foreign currency and nearly 80.0% carried maturities of 3 years or less, resulting in a size-weighted average tenor of 2.9 years.

Figure 5: Market Profile of Outstanding Sustainable Bonds in Viet Nam at the End of June 2024

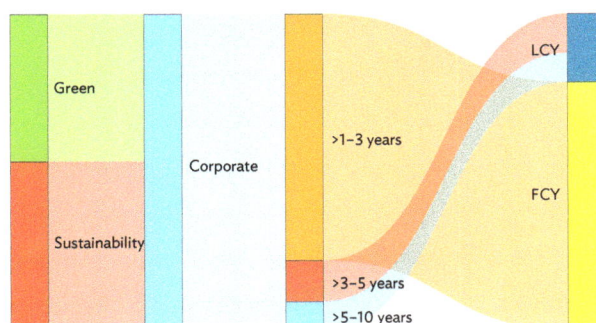

FCY = foreign currency, LCY = local currency.
Source: *AsianBondsOnline* calculations based on Bloomberg LP data.